Making Sense of Play

Making Sense of Play

Supporting children in their play

Perry Else

Open University Press

Open University Press
McGraw-Hill Education
McGraw-Hill House
Shoppenhangers Road
Maidenhead
Berkshire
England
SL6 2QL

email: enquiries@openup.co.uk
world wide web: www.openup.co.uk

and Two Penn Plaza, New York, NY 10121-2289, USA

First published 2014

A catalogue record of this book is available from the British Library

ISBN-13: 978-0-33-524710-3 (pb)
ISBN-10: 0-33-524710-5 (pb)
eISBN: 978-0-33-524711-0

Library of Congress Cataloging-in-Publication Data
CIP data applied for

Typesetting and e-book compilations by
RefineCatch Limited, Bungay, Suffolk

Praise for this book

"Perry Else's book, Making Sense of Play, *is just what we might expect from one of the UK's leading playwork authors. Drawing extensively on Else's work with a number of theorists, it is thought provoking in its content and challenging in the breadth of its scope. Those of us who value diagrams and tables as a mechanism for clarifying complex concepts will be rewarded by the format of the chapters. I recommend this book to anyone with an analytical preference, and an interest in the way societies cater for the needs of children at play."*

Fraser Brown, Professor of Playwork,
Leeds Beckett University, UK

"Perry has the special ability to write a rigorous academic book applying helpful theoretical perspectives to play without ever damaging the precious importance of uninterrupted, spontaneous child-led PLAY."

Sara Knight, Forest School Association and Anglia
Ruskin University, UK

*"*Making Sense of Play *is an accessible and thought-provoking book for all those who are involved or interested in children's play, whether they are practitioners, academics, students or tutors. Written in an engaging and informative manner, it offers opportunities to deepen understanding about different perspectives on play and how this knowledge can aid adults in supporting play. Notably the inclusion of activities and questions for each chapter are invaluable for consolidating understanding and applying the theory to practice."*

Julia Sexton, Senior Lecturer in Childhood Studies,
Sheffield Hallam University, UK

To the people who help make each moment playful, as always Mary, Millie and Ethan.

> You never need to doubt it
> I'll make you so sure about it
> God only knows what I'd be without you
> *Brian Wilson and Tony Asher 1966*

Contents

Acknowledgements

This book would not have been written without the support of many people; these are ones that helped most.

Gordon Sturrock – the journey goes on, but even with a bumpy road, playing is what makes it extraordinary; thanks for always being challenging, graceful and playful.

For contributions conscious and unconscious, acknowledged and forgotten, for inspiring and challenging others, then and now – HRB Bob Hughes.

With thanks for endless cups of reflective tea, sharing stories and poking me once in a while, Julia Sexton.

Beth Cooper, the circus runaway with a big heart, who gets it.

'A kind heart is a fountain of gladness, making everything in its vicinity freshen into smiles' – *Washington Irving* could have been talking about Joanna Philpot.

Sam Humberstone-Bielby for being the cover boy, and blue through and through.

All the consciously caring and considerate staff working in the Royal Hallamshire Hospital, Sheffield; I would not have been able to do this without you all, thank you.

Thanks to the National Children's Bureau for permission to quote from *A Journey Not a Destination* (NCB 2010), originally prepared by the author, with Julia Sexton and Eddie Nuttall.

1

What is play?

- Imagine – a child on a dark, winter's night running past the house of 'the bogeyman', screaming at the top of her voice.
- Imagine – a child walking through a park, stopping for a moment to watch the soft fall of hailstones though the streetlight's sodium beam.
- Imagine – a child pretending to be a music conductor, leading an imaginary orchestra to a recorded piece of music. With his mother as audience, the child is one minute acting gruff and serious, the next light and frivolous, until finally he collapses in a heap of giggles at the nonsense of it all.

Three moments; each different to the other, each with different energy levels, actions and settings – yet each able to be described as *play*. Often when talking about play and playing, we experience a paradox – the spirit of playfulness in these moments has similar elements that we recognize as play, yet the experience/play event itself can be very different. Also while the spirit of playfulness may be similar, the quality of playfulness may change from person to person depending on their ability, awareness and experience.

This chapter will explore different definitions of play, before working towards a clear definition for us to use. There then follows a list of the *Essential Characteristics of Playing*, and some key elements that help with identifying and supporting play. The final section explains how to use the book and what the chapters will cover.

Definitions of play

To begin at the beginning (and the middle and the end) . . . Play is a process.

Many people have attempted to define what 'play' is, and the arguments come thick and fast. One definition says it is fun, another points out that play is often too serious to be fun. One author says that play is future focused and about learning skills, another that play is 'in the moment' for whatever the player wants at that time.

In this sense we are talking about the mostly spontaneous, *self-chosen* play of children (though not only children). In modern English, the word *play* has many connotations: make-believe, having fun, engaging in a game, competing in a game, taking a role in a team, taking a role on stage, performing music, operating a device for recorded music, describing light or water when moving irregularly, teasing, gambling or speculating in some enterprise. Some definitions may describe children when they are playing, though many explain activities that are only part playful; some describe actions that have nothing to do with the play of children.

So, to be clear, in this book we are looking to explore the mostly spontaneous, open, unbounded and potentially limitless play of children.

Play and playwork writers have over the years identified the characteristics that define the qualities of play according to their own value systems. That is, developmentalists have seen play as a means of learning, biologists as a way of using the body, sociologists as means of social interaction. Play tended to be described in terms of what it was thought to achieve or develop, rather than for its particular characteristics.

The writer Jean Piaget (1896–1980) considered play an 'essential element in the normal development' of children. Piaget is known for his proposition that there were clear stages to a child's development that each child passed through at critical ages; describing these in play terms, they were: sensorimotor, or sensory/physical play, symbolic play, 'putting things together' and play with rules. While Piaget has been very influential, especially with young children's educators, more recent thinkers have realized that development is not so predictable and prefer to see it as continuous, lifelong activity.

Theorists coming from a biological perspective saw play as a means of exercising the body for amusement, or to use up 'surplus energy'. Friedrich Schiller (1759–1805) had the opinion that when animals had no need to find food or defend themselves from predators, they spent energy in 'aimless activity'. In modern times, theorists have recognized that regularly using and exercising our bodies has useful health benefits, and that play may be a way of developing healthy habits to help prevent obesity later in life.

Lev Vygotsky (1896–1934) showed that social and cognitive developments were not separate, and that the one supported the other. He said that children's lives were influenced by their friends, families and communities. More of a behaviouralist than Piaget, he believed that communication and interaction were vital to children's construction of knowledge, and that through play children were capable of 'behaving beyond their age, above their usual everyday behaviour'. Vygotsky coined the phrase Zone of Proximal Development (ZPD), the skills that children could learn from peers or adults, if close to their current skill level; if the step was too great the child may not understand or be able to process the change.

Bob Hughes (1944–), when talking about evolutionary play (2012: 14), stated that, 'Play is critically important to human development and evolution'; he showed that the drive to play, while serving physiological, biological ends, also contributes to our mastery of the environment and our bodies, and our development of higher-level thinking and imagination. Gerald Edelman (1929–) explained that human knowledge arose with changes in brain size and function, 'And that once language emerged in human evolution, our knowledge and its development, as well as our evolutionary path, depended on culture' (2006: 55).

While these perspectives could be explored in depth, the view taken in this book is that, while play emerged during evolutionary development to serve biological purposes that lent some advantage, it now serves additional functions in the understanding of ourselves in relation to others and the environment around us. Thus the function of play for children is neither solely genetically defined nor emergent from the culture in which the child is raised; it is an interesting and complex result of both.

Towards a clear definition of play

We could go on, but to see if there was any consensus on what play is, the key ingredients of play, and to arrive at a definition for this book, an analysis was made of definitions by varied theorists and practitioners (including Garvey, Bekoff, Brown, Bruce, Burghardt, Cohen, Hughes and King, Kilvington, Mainemelis and Ronson, Pellegrini and Russell – see Appendix 1, discussed in Chapter 2). Some of these argue the biological purpose of play; others use a psychological or cultural rationale.

To take just a few examples, Catherine Garvey (1977) listed the characteristics of play as pleasurable or enjoyable, spontaneous and voluntary, with no extrinsic goals, involving some active engagement on the part of the player and with 'certain systematic relations to what is not play' – i.e. it might have the actions of work but it's not really. Bob Hughes and Frank King (1984) said that play is a process; that the way of playing was important, not what children play with. They claimed that play was freely chosen by the player, was personally directed, with the manner of playing decided by the child, and that play was engaged in for its own sake; the impulse to play coming from within. Tina Bruce (2001) identified 12 features of play, some of which describe the actions of play, though others illustrate what she saw as the purpose of play. Bruce said that children choose to play and cannot be made to play; they make up rules as they play and thereby keep control of their play, and when playing have a 'personal agenda'. She also spoke about children 'rehearsing the future' in their role-play, trying out their most recent learning, skills and competencies, pretending though play, and that they play alone sometimes and sometimes with other children.

While not the whole of the story, this analysis was an attempt to identify the most common elements from the work of those theorists and practitioners. From that analysis, and using previous work, the list of the Essential Characteristics of Playing has been prepared (see Table 1.1). The more of these characteristics that are present when an individual is playing, the more we can be confident that the person *is* 'playing'.

This is an interesting (and admittedly personal) list – and while it contains many recognizable characteristics that we could say contribute to a playful experience, the list by itself does not describe all that is play; play really is one of those things that is greater than the sum of its parts.

The first characteristic is included to remind us that *how* play is carried out is more important than what is done; many writers in the modern era seem to have taken a lead from Susanna Millar: 'Perhaps play is best used as an adverb; not as a name of a class of activities, nor as distinguished by the accompanying mood, but to describe how and under what conditions an action is performed' (Millar 1968: 21).

Gregory Bateson (1991: 203) also considered play not to be a description of a particular action but as a *class* of actions, 'to be classified together in accordance with the organism's vision of the context in which he/she is acting.'

Gordon Sturrock (2011) took this point further; 'Play does not have many definitions/functions: it has only one. It is a singularity. The sole purpose of play is to induce PLAYING'. This goes to the heart of why we play; play knows no boundaries or limits, we play to experience playing (the benefits of the activity will be discussed later). We can see that play is inherently *neophilic* – that it helps players find new things – but the fields or frames in which we play

Table 1.1 The essential characteristics of playing.

1. Play is a process, not a specific action
2. Self-chosen, with a willingness to participate
3. Active engagement, attentive response to feedback
4. Sufficiently safe, physically and psychologically
5. A whole body/mind experience
6. Timelessness, lost in the moment
7. Curiosity; attracted to newness or new experiences
8. Pleasurable
9. Different for each person
10. Satisfaction is self-defined, with no extrinsic goals

can vary immensely and it is only when we perceive the frame that we can label the play as one thing or another: social play or communication play or imaginary play. Play can last seconds or continue as a theme for years. As we grow older many people have special friends who can pick up the game whenever they meet, be it months or years apart; with such people, it is as if the 'invitation to play' is always on the table.

Many people claim to know what play is when they see it, and many adults and parents will recognize playfulness when it happens, so why do we need a list of play characteristics and how might practitioners in play benefit from having such a list? Well to say that play is a way of doing things only takes us so far. It reminds us that play is not predictable, does not fit in a clear 'subject box' and is difficult to initiate in humans who do not want to play. But it also means that what is perceived as playful is also in the eye of the observer; unless we are careful, the observer (usually an adult) decides that something is not playful and intervenes to curtail or stop the child's play. Having a list of the characteristics of play helps us notice the child is playing and that we should not get in the way. In no way should these descriptions be read as predictive of children's behaviour – like all humans, that behaviour belongs to them and cannot be anticipated as it is affected by too many factors within the child, others and the environment.

If we see an activity that appears to be playful, we can check to see if the other characteristics are present. Are the children taking part willingly, do they have a choice to leave or stay? Are they responsive to what is happening in the play? Do they exhibit a 'play face' or playful actions – with smiles and high levels of energy – or do they look worried or bored? Do they seem to be engrossed in the play with their thoughts and actions working in harmony? Are they doing something new or in a new way; does it seem satisfying or pleasurable? Does the child decide when to stop the play and move on to something else, or does someone else force them to stop? Play will of course be different for each person, even those playing together, for each perspective and set of experiences will be different. We should not expect that games and activities produce the same outcomes for everyone alike. If we are to support children in their play we need to observe their play and try to determine what is happening. Later, in Chapter 5, *Interacting with playing children*, we will look at this in some depth, but for now note that asking some of these questions will take us closer to knowing when play is happening.

Key elements of play

To help practitioners identify quickly when children are playing, the ten characteristics listed in Table 1.1 have been distilled into three key elements in the following formula:

play = choice + engagement + satisfaction

Table 1.2 The key elements of playing.

Self-chosen, willingly participating	• Sufficiently safe, physically and psychologically
Active **engagement**, responding attentively to what is happening	• A whole-body/mind experience • Timelessness, lost in the moment • Curiosity; attracted to newness or new experiences
Satisfaction defined by the player, with no extrinsic goals	• Play is a process, not a thing • Pleasurable • Different for each person

When children are seen to be playing, are they willingly participating – have they chosen to be in the activity? Are they engaged, responding attentively to what is happening? And is satisfaction defined by the player or determined by someone outside the game? These three questions may remind us of the other characteristics, as shown in Table 1.2.

These key elements can be seen to be important for the qualities they generate in the playing child, as follows.

- Choice helps the child understand the concept of 'self' and free will; that actions and events follow from the expression of choice, that there are consequences both pleasurable and painful.

- Engagement creates a sense of focus and involvement, helping children persevere and strive for the pleasure of the activity, and may help with understanding delayed gratification; that a task worked at can be rewarding in a different way to one easily won.

- Satisfaction is likely to help with a sense of reward in the moment. When playing, children do it for 'now', not for a future return. Satisfaction through play creates a sense of aliveness not often present in other modes of being.

With this definition in mind, we can go on to make sense of play, looking at how it affects children, how adults might support it, and how we might examine and assess settings for their playfulness.

Questions to help practitioners put the ideas into their work with playing children

Start by looking for the Key Elements of Playing – choice, engagement and satisfaction; can they be seen when watching children play? How do others see these elements in children? Are the cues always the same?

Make a checklist using the ten Essential Characteristics of Playing. Choose a quiet corner to observe the children playing and tick off the characteristics when you see them. Which are easiest to spot, which most difficult? How might what you see be misunderstood by other adults?

Find a play definition of your own and compare it with the ten Essential Characteristics of Playing. What is similar, what is different? Does the language used in the definition you found suggest a child-centred or adult-centred approach to practice?

How to use the book

When making sense of play; it is helpful to test theory with practice, and reflect on practice using established (and emerging) theory. Theories are useful to help us make sense of the world, but they cannot entirely predict or control it; reality has a habit of being quirky and unpredictable despite our best efforts. As play is a very mobile phenomenon, a way of doing things, it is necessary when working with children in their play to reflect often on what we have been doing and what we have observed in children. These reflections and observations can then help us plan our work and hopefully improve our practice. In each chapter there are questions to help with applying the ideas and tools being discussed, using them in different environments with different children, and hopefully changing the tools or ourselves to produce a better outcome for children.

Figure 1.1 illustrates how to use this book using an adapted version of Kolb and Fry's learning process (1975): doing something, evaluating it, ideally thinking about theory before planning how to implement changes or carry out further practice. Of course the process can start anywhere, but the format of this book starts with theory, both established and developing. The first three chapters discuss theory. Chapter 2 aims to draw together many views and forms of play in a holistic model, the Integral Play Framework (Else 1999, 2009); readers of *The Value of Play* (Else 2009) may be familiar with some of the material in this section. Chapter 3 will use the Integral Play Framework to make sense of others' views on play. A number of significant theories and approaches are explored to help practitioners increase their awareness and understanding. What do different theories offer; does the theorist's perspective have an effect on what is included (and what is left out)? Chapter 3 also takes the Integral Play Framework further and shows how, while a simple model, it is holistic at all levels, yet hopefully with no judgement about the 'stage' at which children may be at; no 'levels' are better or worse than others. There will be an explanation of the skills needed to be a mindful, self-reflective practitioner.

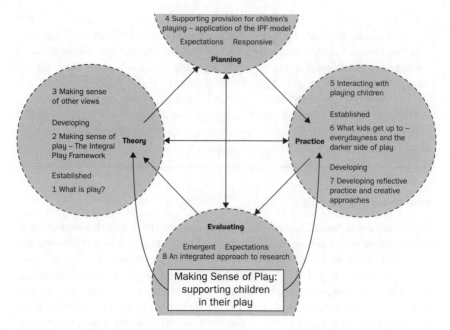

Figure 1.1 Making sense of this book.

We will then move onto making plans for supporting children's play in Chapter 4. It is argued that supporting children's playing provision should be based on the needs of the child, as delivered by the worker, through the provision and within the laws and policies of the city/country. In supporting playing children we will need to be aware of our and the children's expectations of the provision, and yet still responsive to the ideas and actions that arise day to day in the setting. We will aim to make play provision that meets the many and varied demands that children put upon it and us in a helpful and inclusive manner.

Chapters 5 to 7 will look at practice, aiming to understand playing children and exploring what they get up to in their play, especially some of the routine, everyday and darker aspects of play. Looking at interactions with children is the subject of Chapter 5, when we will explore the Play Cycle – drive, cue, frame, flow, return, etc. – in depth. There will be an explanation of psycholudics, 'the study of the mind and psyche at play', aiming to describe the process of play as it happens (Sturrock, as cited in Sturrock and Else 1998), describing key terms with examples. Often when talking about children's play, writers tend to emphasize the ideal states of play for the child and the environment, yet quite frequently in their spontaneous play, children are not in ideal states or conditions – things just happen, they react to the playfulness of a space or they play in ways that others consider to be inappropriate.

Chapter 6 will explore these ways of playing, looking at the individual and cultural aspects of play as well as the physical and social manifestations. The issues of play deprivation and 'deep play' will be explored. Reflecting on our work is the focus of Chapter 7, where we explore the 'best' approach to take, trying to identify what gets in the way of reflection and what tools can we use day to day and through our career to help us develop better practice. We will then explore ways of enhancing playfulness and creativity for us. We will also compare the traits of creativity to those of play, with a brief look at common blockages.

Chapter 8 will show how the Integral Play Framework tool has been used in a national evaluation of playwork provision, in setting-based research to test the validity of practice, and in the business world to assess the quality of play spaces. Methodology and methods for evaluation will be discussed in some depth.

As the main model for the rest of the book, let's begin with an explanation of the *Integral Play Framework*.

2

Making sense of play: the Integral Play Framework

To begin making sense of play, let's start with a story . . .

Once upon a time, long ago in the *abundant land,* or Ireland as it is now known, there was a mighty chieftain. This was no ordinary chieftain for as well as being a strong warrior, he was also something of a poet, a philosopher and a seer. The chieftain ruled his land fairly and with justice, and his name was *Fionn MacCumhaill* – known in English as Finn McCool. It was said that during Finn's reign a young child with a rich jewel in her hand could walk from the north to the south of the land and not be touched. When not defending Ireland, killing giants or gaining all the knowledge in the world, Finn would spend his time writing poetry, talking about the meaning of life or hunting.

One afternoon, after a busy morning's hunting, Finn and his gang stopped for a meal and a bit of chat. Like Finn, many of his warriors were poets and philosophers; one of them asked a question, 'What is the most beautiful sound in the world?'

The first to answer was a stout warrior, who said, 'The sound of swords crashing against shields.'

The next was a romantic who said, 'The sound of a couple in love.'

The third was a father; 'A newborn baby's cry is the most beautiful sound in the world.'

'No, no,' exclaimed the next, who was a devout man, 'It's the sound of church bells calling us to mass.'

The last to speak was a hedonist, a pleasure seeker, who argued that the most beautiful sound in the world was, 'Heavily laden plates landing on the dinner table.'

The arguments continued for a while until the warriors realized that they could not reach agreement, and so they turned to Finn for an answer.

Finn, who was lying on his back gazing at the clouds gliding across the sky, paused for a moment, took a straw out of his mouth and said, 'The most beautiful sound in the world is the sound of what is happening Now; the sound of life.'

The argument in this story is a lot like the debates around the meaning of play – different people see different things in it, each according to their own perspective. Active people see play as physical activity, its purpose is to get children running around, using their bodies or using up surplus energy. Thinkers will see children solving problems in their play. Artists will recognize the creative aspects of play in how children assemble thoughts and things. Managers will notice how children negotiate in their play, and choose roles or delegate to others. How children learn through play might be noted by teachers; and how they form small groups and work alone could be seen by sociologists. Lots of different adults, lots of different opinions. And of course if we ask children, they will be a lot like Finn; for when children are playing they usually do it for what it offers 'Now' – the pleasure and satisfaction of actually playing, with little concern about how it might improve their well-being or their cognitive reasoning. So how do we make sense of play?

Sports people and biologists focus on the physical manifestations of play; how playing uses and affects muscles and bodily tissue, how the actions humans make shape ourselves and the things around us. Thinkers and teachers recognize the cognitive benefits of play, and how play is both of the mind and how it shapes the mind. Anthropologists will see echoes in play of ritual, customs and festivals. Mathematicians will see children counting things, controlling data and working out strategies and probabilities in their play. Those interested in roles and power will see play as contest or about sorting roles; who's in charge and who's doing the work.

> Developmental science has been influenced more and more by an appreciation of the profound and multi-layered interrelations between the 'intellect' (our cognitive abilities), 'heart' (emotions and motivation), 'eyes and ears' (perception), human spirit, physical body, social relations, and culture. A full understanding requires attention to all of these multiply-interrelated facets.
>
> *Adele Diamond (2007: 152)*

This chapter will explain the Integral Play Framework (Else 1999, 2009), how it is holistic in its description of play, yet does not attempt to predict any types of play. The benefits of play are explained using various sources, and a description of a possible evolution of playfulness concludes the chapter.

The Integral Play Framework

The Integral Play Framework (Else 1999, 2009) is one model that explains how these differing views can be drawn together in a holistic description that recognizes them as different but equal. Adapting the work of Ken Wilber (1997), who constructed a model that explains and integrates different perspectives about the human condition, the Integral Play Framework aims to explain and integrate varied views on play. The framework integrates several perspectives and shows how they link together; the comments are based on 15 years' development of the model, using observations from practice and with playing children.

As human animals, we exist in the world as bodies in space and also as minds within our bodies – one visible, the other invisible; one real, the other insubstantial. Yet what we think affects our bodies and how our bodies feel affects our mind. And also influencing our human condition is our relationship with others. Often we perceive ourselves as alone – 'No one else feels the way I feel' – but we live in relation to everyone around us; we are at least the product of two other people – our mother and father. We behave differently when alone to how we act when with others; we may have shared or wildly divergent views, we may choose to work together or fight to get what we want. These aspects of human life Wilber (1997) describes as the four quadrants, each explaining part of what it is to be in existence. The four quadrants, and how these relate to play, are shown in Figure 2.1.

It is important when looking at the model to realize that the four quadrants are dynamic and that each aspect influences all the others: 'how I feel affects my behaviour, my relationships will influence my thoughts and actions' – the circles are intended to remind us of that connection. We can see how the Body and Physical World quadrant would be the main domain of biologists and physicists. The Mind quadrant could be explained by psychologists, psychiatrists and those interested in cognition. Anthropologists would be interested in cultural ritual, customs and festivals; sociologists would combine both Culture and Society in their studies. Developmentalists could be attracted to either cognitive development or physical development and levels of well-being, depending on their interests. Other examples could be used (and will be explored in Chapter 3, *Making sense of other views*) but it is possible to see how the framework aims to describe the full human experience.

Forming the whole

Wilber conceived of the model as a *holarchy* (after Koestler 1967). A holarchy is a hierarchy of *holons*; a holon is complete in itself but also part of something else. So the four quadrants each describe part of what it is to be human yet come together to form the whole. There are 'levels' to the framework

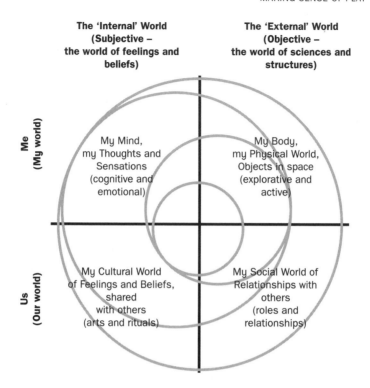

Figure 2.1 The Integral Play Framework.

Source: Else, after Wilber (1997).

where at the centre of the model things are generally smaller and simpler, and towards the edges they are larger and more complex. In the objective world, an atom is complete in itself and is part of a molecule, which is part of a cell; an arm is complete in itself and is part of a child; a child is complete and is part of a family, a family is part of a community, and so on. In the subjective world, thoughts may be instinctual, emotional, symbolic, conceptual and rational; belief systems may be 'magical' as with toddlers, aggressive as in dominating, ordered – following the rules, competitive, non-competitive, and so on. And just so, muscular movement is part of locomotor play, which may be part of dramatic or rough and tumble play.

The relationship between holons at different levels is not intended to be read as a 'pecking order', and can just as meaningfully be related with terms like 'made up of' or 'part of', as of 'higher or lower'. In relation to humans, Spangler defines holarchy as follows: 'In a hierarchy, participants can be compared and evaluated on the basis of position, rank, relative power, seniority and the like. But in a holarchy each person's value comes from their individuality and uniqueness and the capacity to engage and interact with others' (Spangler 2008). Similarly with play; play is led by the player – they will do what they want to do at a particular time according to their skills, knowledge, ability and mood. Where possible no external judgement should be assigned or implied, as to do so might affect the play or our response to it.

The concept of the holarchy as well as aiming to be holistic is also progressive; different skills may be developed though experience and will include simpler versions of themselves. Interpersonal skills may include getting on with strangers, but will also encompass getting on with friends and family members – 'social play is a form of social learning' (Konner 2010: 512); the skill of bonding with parents is not lost as friendship groups are formed. The levels of the holarchy do not need to be read as 'better' when things become more complicated; each person, each child, will have the skills, attitudes and values that suit their life and their experience to date. Each individual will adapt to the world they find themselves in; Inuit children find that using a sharp knife is essential to eating well; Korowai children become used to living in tree tops as soon as they can walk; UK children expect that being driven in a car is the best way to get to school.

The framework also shows the need for an integrated approach to play and provision for children. Adults tend to make provision for children according to the dominant patterns within each quadrant or domain: sports people will emphasize movement, agility, balance and coordination; artists support appreciation and skills for creative projects; some value logical, mathematical skills, some literacy skills, others interpersonal and leadership skills. However, children need, now even more than ever, to have a balance of abilities across the four domains, to use their bodies well in a variety of ways, to feel and be able to express their emotions, be connected and included into the places and communities where they live, and to understand how groups and collectives work so that they can make the necessary and vital contributions necessary to enjoy and sustain lives – their own and others.

'The map is not the territory'

Looking at the Integral Play Framework from a human perspective, we can simply group our skill sets into those shown in Figure 2.2: for example, Gross Physical Movements; Agility, Balance, Coordination; Roles and Leadership; Morals and Respect; Emotional Awareness and Control; Logical Skills. These skill areas are similar to the 'multiple intelligences' proposed by Gardner (1999), who argued that the traditional view of intelligence as seen in the west was too limited, being focused as it was on logical and linguistic intelligence. As important as thinking and symbolic aptitudes are, they are not much use if you need to run away from a predator, act in a show or sing a song. As we

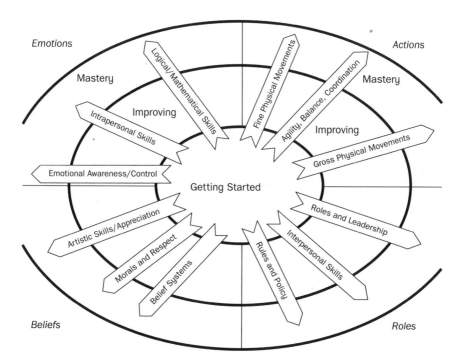

Figure 2.2 Developing holistically.

grow these skill sets move from Getting Started though Improving to Mastery, if we are fortunate and have the ideal forms of support and experience.

Like all models, this framework is best read as a descriptor of observed behaviours and experienced patterns; while it helps describe actions and feelings it does not predict or control them. While we can see certain activities as 'typical' or 'realistic' they should not be read as activities that *must* occur when children play. For example, while a toddler might act on instinct or emotion, and 'believe' in 'peek-a-boo', they will not explain their actions in words or by explaining rules. Yet an older child or adult, while understanding rules or theories of behaviour might still act on instinct or with a desire to dominate (or act submissively). We should also remember that individual children will not 'follow the rules' – this is not an 'ages and stages' model, where change when it occurs is seen as an extension of what happened before. Children can surprise themselves (and adults) by doing things out of the ordinary or with a surprising degree of maturity, or we may have 'gifted' children who are skilled in one area 'above their years' – or we may have children that for whatever reasons may stay where they are, through choice, fear, complacency, understanding or physical aptitude.

The Integral Play Framework helps adults providing for play to realize that children need spaces that meet all their play needs, physical as well as relational, cognitive and creative as well as cultural. Adults who support children's play should give them spaces to run around, resources to express themselves, a chance to be in a group and alone, the opportunity to work things through at their own pace and in their own way. This is explained in detail later in Chapter 5, *Interacting with playing children*.

Play is unpredictable

When we understand that play is not simply about cognitive development or physical activity but a combination and enhancement of both (as well as other things), we can begin to see that *how* children play is the most important factor here. It is the way of action that makes something playful, not the activity itself (Sylva *et al.* 1976). Therefore when children are playing they will be choosing what to play with and how to play; exploring sand might be a construction activity or a social activity with a friend – or both at the same time. When a child is engaged in an activity they may be doing it for the pleasure it offers in the moment, not because of any external or projected outcome. And when they choose to end an activity it is because something else is more attractive or because the activity has met their needs for the time being.

> A child may be in a reverie, a daydream, watching the wind blow through leaves or tall grass; suddenly with a tap on the shoulder she is off chasing a friend. While running along, she picks up a stick to use as rocket or whip for an imaginary horse, then tags her friend and runs away to hide. When the friend finds her, they stop the tag game and start an informal game of pretend where the stick has now become a witch's broom . . . and so on.

As adults we might describe these activities as perceptual play, locomotor play, object play, symbolic archetypal play (see 'Play types', Chapter 3 and Appendix 2) and so on, but to the child it is 'just playing'. She did not consciously decide to play 'according to the rules', but went with the flow of the game, making choices and decisions as things occurred to her, stopping and starting activities as the moment took her. And these actions, while not undertaken for any deliberate outcome, will have been helping her brain make connections between concepts and actions, helping her body become more flexible and stronger, and helping her get on with her friend. The actions may even have helped with learning about the nature of the world and using materials in new ways, but she will have been learning informally and not because it was expected of her, nor to any adult curriculum. Children in their play may repeat activities over and over again, developing skill and mastery in the activity, or they may take an activity to its extreme. Examples include children who collect things and want more and more of the same (though slightly different) thing, in order to play similar but different games and activities. Or the child who 'pushes things to the limit' – be that jumping higher and higher on a trampoline until they fall off, making the plastic brick tower higher and higher until it falls over, or questioning a brother/sister/mother until they get told off. These actions will be understandably risky, not just in a physical sense but in that actions may not always result in success. By making mistakes and trying again, children will be learning to be resilient, resistant to failure and quick to recover when things do not always go as planned.

The Integral Play Framework explains how children can play in different ways and how those actions will impact in the different domains to bring physical, social, cognitive and emotional benefits to children; play – as a process and not just simple activity – helps the brain become more effective, helps children develop skills and understanding, contributing directly to good physical and mental well-being, and is also satisfying while it is occurring.

The benefits of play

The evidence of the direct benefits of play for children and others has been established; it is 'of the moment', and gives immediate pleasure and satisfaction, it helps develop stronger cortical links in the brain, helps with informal learning and creativity, as well as providing important physical exercise (see Lester and Russell 2010). The benefits of playing, while they may be assessed as outcomes (as has been the desire of many governments), are the product of the self-chosen activities that children engage in – it is therefore important that the play process is supported so that children are able to interact freely as they want with those elements that interest them. If the process is interrupted, curtailed or controlled by others, then the playing may also be interrupted, curtailed or controlled and so not be fully playful – or fully beneficial.

'Stronger cortical links in the brain'

There is now strong evidence that one reason for the evolution of playing is to help develop more efficient brains by enhancing cortical connections; that when we play, the nerve signals our bodies generate create pathways in the brain that help with brain development (Edelman 2006; Pellis and Pellis 2009). The brain expands in volume four times from birth to the teenage years, and brain structure and function in adults are products of both evolution and individual development (Johnson 2008). So the brain has elements that are determined by genetics and biology, yet full growth is supported by environment and activity. Smith (2010: 217) quotes Panksepp as saying 'play is quintessentially capable of activating the very best that the [brain] is capable of'.

Furthermore, 'The brain is a self-organising and adaptive system. It is self-organizing in the sense that at most stages of development it selects appropriate input for its own further development' (Johnson 2008: 5), and the brain is attracted to new activities and 'tasks at which [children] are only partially successful, and motivated to persist until they have achieved mastery'. It is as if the brain directs the growing children to seek out new experiences and new ways of doing things, and these varied activities help build stronger links in the brain. Pink supports this desire for new experiences – *neophilia* – 'Our basic nature is to be curious and self-directed' – and if as adults we are 'passive and inert, that's not because it's our nature. It's because something flipped our default setting' (2010: 89). Of course not all such activities can be described as playful, yet those that are self-chosen and pleasurable tend to be described as play.

'Helps with informal learning and creativity'

A lot has been written about play as a means to learn, or 'learning through play', yet Burghardt says that play contributes to developing 'effective systems for learning' rather than particular learning outcomes (2005, quoted in Lester and Russell 2008: 128). And playing in detailed and involved ways improves how children learn, as Fantuzzo and others suggest that children who are successful at playing with friends show greater cognitive, social and physical abilities than others less skilful (quoted in Lester and Russell 2008: 128). In contrast to those adults who feel they must set programmes to guide play, Pollard lends force to the argument that self-chosen activity is better for children; 'Only children themselves can make sense, understand and learn' (quoted in Bruce 2006: 181).

Choice is also important for creativity; Pink is very clear on the point; 'intrinsic motivation – the drive to do something because it is interesting, challenging and absorbing – is essential for high levels of creativity' (2010: 46). In play children will experiment with the 'how', the 'what' and the 'why'; questioning everything and trying new ways of doing and being and feeling. In their early years children can be very creative, though some seem to lose that capability as they grow older and as they play less; if we are intrinsically *neophilic* or curious then self-chosen play will help children satisfy that drive for newness, and bring them pleasure and help them see things in a new way.

'Providing important physical exercise'

The connection of play to physical movement and skills is obvious to many, and research suggests that providing important physical exercise helps develop endurance, control of body movements and perceptual-motor integration (Lester and Russell 2010). Equally, several studies have shown that not being active in early life tends towards obesity in later life (Cassidy *et al.* 2010; National Obesity Observatory 2013). The benefits of improved physical fitness, coordination, balance and agility have been reported from playing and moving in spaces offering challenge and unpredictability (Fjortoft 2004). Active play supports a dynamic range of movements, and varied challenges with irregular and unpredictable patterns increase and strengthen heart rate and blood flow (Yun *et al.* 2005).

'Immediate pleasure and satisfaction'

The quality of *nowness* and being in the moment reminds us that 'the most beautiful sound in the world' was defined as, 'What is happening Now; the sound of life'. Children certainly seem to be full of life when they are playing.

Play is 'of the moment', and gives pleasure and satisfaction to the player at the time they are playing; children who are unhappy or frustrated are unlikely to be playing. Pleasure and satisfaction are used to describe children's affect (their emotional response) rather than 'fun' or 'happy' because many play activities may be quiet, involved, complex or thoughtful – examples include drawing, building, making stories, solving problems. The pleasure is evident in the 'a-ha!' moment at varied times in the activity, or in the satisfaction of getting a sandcastle to stand up or a kite to fly. The pleasure of play has been recognized as contributing to many things; feeling good helps with 'flexible thinking and problem solving, mastery and optimism' (Pressman and Cohen 2005; Frederickson 2006; Izen and Reeve 2006; all cited in Lester and Russell 2008: 128). Seligman (2002: 39) states that, 'high energy positive emotions like joy make people playful, and play is deeply implicated in the building of physical resources'. It is also recognized that positive emotions can help with both physical and psychological health issues by promoting resilience, endurance and optimism (Salovey *et al.* 2000; cited in Lester and Russell 2008: 128).

In the next chapter we will look at how the Integral Play Framework can help explain how varied views on play may have emerged. However, the Framework also suggests how these benefits may be linked. A summary of the benefits of play (Table 2.1) shows how different views all contribute to the various types of play adults see in children and the many outcomes that are anticipated from the behaviour. (While terms have been placed in specific columns for clarity, they should not be read as prescriptive; children will play how they may, as described above; the table is intended to show how different views may be linked and reconciled. And all play types may include aspects of each characteristic – e.g. rough and tumble play includes elements of planning and communication, yet is primarily physical.)

Children can play primarily using their bodies (running around), using their minds (thinking and problem solving) or with others (communicating

Table 2.1 Summary of the benefits of play.

Generic type of behaviour	Reptilian	Mammalian	Human
Core focus	Body	Body/mind	Mind
Immediate feeling/response	Somatic	Somatic/interpersonal	Intrapersonal
Brain area and structure (Johnson 2008)	Archipallium/hippocampus/limbic	Paleopallium/limbic/allocortex	Neopallium/neocortex
Multiple intelligences (Gardner 1999)	Visual – spatial	Interpersonal	Logical – mathematical
	Bodily – kinaesthetic	Verbal – linguistic	Intrapersonal
		Musical – rhythmic and harmonic	Existential
		Naturalistic	
Nowness/in the moment/'beingness'	Sensation	Feeling	Thought
		Emotion	Spirit
Play types (Else, after Hughes 1996a)	Exploratory play	Communication play	Emotional play
	Impulsive play	Dramatic play	Symbolic play
	Perceptual play	Family play	Creative play
	Object play	Group play	Symbolic conceptual play
	Locomotor play	Symbolic archetypal play	Creative cognitive play
	Rough and tumble play	Role-play	Creative artistic play
	Sexual play	Social play	Fantasy play
		Socio-dramatic play	Imaginative play
			Mastery play
			Deep play
			Global play
Recapitulative play (Hall 1904, cited in Hughes 2012; Spencer 1904)	Hunting/survival	Caring/communication	Symbols/creativity/innovation
Longer-term benefits/ 'becomingness'	Physical well-being	Social well-being	Mental well-being
	Muscular growth	Belongingness	Brain elasticity
	Flexibility/agility	Social connections	Resilience
	Coordination	Acceptance	Autonomy

and bonding); these forms of play also coincide with forms that are shown in other species. Recapitulation Theory (Hall 1904, cited in Hughes 2012; Spencer 1904) suggests that playing helps children to repeat earlier human evolutionary stages.

The evolution of playfulness

Humans are not the only species to exhibit playful behaviours – so playing with experiences (given enough spare time and resources) must have begun quite early in animal development; play 'affects biological evolution by enabling organisms to adapt rapidly to novel environments' (Bateson and Martin 2013: 1). Play clearly occurs in animals other than higher mammals and humans, and just as clearly the forms of play are different and yet serve similar purposes – striving for continued existence in the world from that animal's perspective – and so serving vital biological, physiological purposes. The repetition and practice elements of play may have conferred an evolutionary advantage, especially when nerve cells and complex brains emerged. It has been shown (Siviy and Atrens 1992) that play uses up energy and therefore is costly in terms of food acquisition; if an animal is short-lived, the young do not play as much as they are not likely to benefit from play's advantages (Konner 2010: 500).

Burghardt (2005), in his studies about the evolution of playfulness, has made claims that fish and reptiles play; he even claims that wasps can play (yet they cannot play as humans do). It seems reasonable that animals should rehearse responses to certain situations so that if challenged by the environment or threatened by other animals they may have an appropriate response to that situation. Yet the actions of play are very different to those displayed when animals are really threatened, so what is it that animals are preparing for?

Higher animals play willingly within and across species when they feel it is safe to do so, and appear to do this for what may be seen as pleasurable or neophilic/exploratory reasons. It is easy to think of the playful pouncing of kittens and lion cubs, for example, and evidence exists of dogs (as well as other animals) playing with larger and smaller creatures, where clear 'self-limiting' behaviour is taking place (this is where the players limit their actions so as not to cause harm to one another). Polar bears have been shown to play with dogs a tenth of their size for quite extended periods when they could easily kill the smaller animals if they chose (Ladoon n.d.). The playful behaviour is revealed in the exaggerated movements of the animals, with gaping mouths and frisky actions, which are nothing like the 'seriousness' and calm they exhibit when hunting.

While playing and developing practical, physiological benefits, it is likely that behavioural or proto-psychological advantages are increasing at the same time; indeed much research into animal play has been carried out on rats, and in the field on dogs, apes and monkeys, which appears to show this.

Bekoff and Pierce (2009) have written about mammalian animal play across several species and have shown how they exhibit playfulness within their own terms. Bekoff and Pierce (2009) also show that animals display a morality (expressed as care for and protection of other family members), which is another quality that has previously been attributed solely to humans. This makes evolutionary sense; it is unlikely that such a subtle behaviour as morality only came to the fore in humans, or even in apes. It seems clear that a proto-morality must have developed with mammals and pre-mammals. In humans, this behaviour has come to be seen in such complicated concepts as care, compassion, empathy and 'humanity'. Recapitulative play recognizes this evolving playfulness.

Granville Stanley Hall (1904, cited in Hughes 2012) promoted the recapitulation theory of development, based on the principle that growing children would repeat – recapitulate – evolutionary stages of development as they grew up. We can now add to this theory that children will be drawn to light as simple animals are, they will explore the environment and the use of their bodies as animals do. They will find out how to live in nature as early humans did, socialize with others through various play forms, developing more and more complex forms of understanding, until these become symbolic and cognitive; like all animals, they live in the world and try to find their own way through it. Human children are also aware of their awareness of themselves, and can do things just for the fun of it, though the survival skills will take over if the stimulus is strong enough to break into the play frame.

In his discussion on the evolution of play, Konner (2010: 501–502) argued that, while reptiles and amphibians show only rudimentary forms of play, such as pushing repeatedly on floating objects, larger-brained species of birds and mammals play more and with more complexity. Quoting Ewer (1968), Konner stated that, 'The smartest mammals – primates, cetaceans, elephants and carnivores – are the most playful' (2010: 500), with the higher primates, the most intelligent animals being the most playful (2010: 503). Bateson and Martin (2013) concur, differentiating between what they call *play* as recognized by biologists and psychologists (which may be about striving for social dominance) and *playful play* (which has a positive or light-hearted tone). A rudimentary continuum of forms of play is thus indicated, from simple to more complex forms, following the evolution of species from reptiles to mammals to primates to *Homo sapiens* – see Table 2.1. Put simply, there are forms of play associated with moving around and hunting or fleeing, there are forms of play to do with social order and belongingness, and there are forms of play to do with symbolic recognition, metaphor, imagination and 'beingness'. This speculation seems to be supported by *dual process theory* within psychology, where *System 1* is unconscious reasoning, prominent in animals and humans, with responses based on feeling and senses, and *System 2*, or conscious reasoning, where judgements are based on critical examination, and evident mainly in humans and higher animals. Gardner (2008) comments that human brains still operate using survival systems that were necessary thousands of years ago (*System 1*) as well as carefully thought-out strategies that emerged more recently (*System 2*). System 1 feeling-based responses are primal urges and need to make sense of the world before conscious reasoning or *System 2* type thinking emerges; we need to run around and come together socially in groups before we understand symbolic thinking, imagination and self-awareness.

The evolutionary, holistic interaction of play that creates benefits for increased brain plasticity, immediate gratification and help with informal learning and creativity did not come into existence for us yet seems to have reached a pinnacle with humans. The playful actions in the world help shape our brains while they are growing and in critical stages throughout life. The feeling sensations that we get from play cause us to repeat and extend those actions, be they overtly physical, social or creative. These actions and feelings give us opportunities to enjoy and learn from our experiences, trying new ways of doing things in the world or in our imaginations; play has evolved as the species has evolved, from survival skills to group skills to cognitive and emotional skills. The Integral Play Framework gives us a way of describing that journey, while helping us remember how each part is linked to the whole.

Having explored the Integral Play Framework, we will now go on to look at how other people view play.

Questions to help practitioners understand the Integral Play Framework

- Observe children playing for a few minutes; see if you can identify the physical, social, cultural and cognitive elements of their play. How much do they move about? How much do they use their minds? How do they interact with others; do they behave differently with different people?
- Thinking of the four quadrants, can you think of the strengths and weaknesses of each area? Is it good or bad to move around and practise our skills? What happens if we do too much or too little? Is it good or bad to use imaginative play? What are the consequences of too much or too little? How do we feel about social play, culture-based or dramatic play? What 'rules' are we using to form our judgements?
- The Integral Play Framework may be viewed as an extension of Bronfenbrenner's Ecological Systems Theory (1979). Bronfenbrenner argued that the individual affects, and was affected by, the surrounding environment. How do others affect playing children in the four domains, and at various times in their lives? How do children influence and affect others?

3
Making sense of other views

Play is:

'Non-seriousness'

Johan Huizinga

'Pleasurable, enjoyable'

Catherine Garvey

'Directed by the player and voluntary'

Stuart Brown

'Equips the individual with experiences that enable it to meet future challenges in novel ways'

Patrick Bateson and Paul Martin

'About creating a world in which, for that moment, children are in control and can seek out uncertainty in order to triumph over it'

Stuart Lester and Wendy Russell

'What I do when everyone else has stopped telling me what to do'

Michael Follett, though often attributed to Anonymous Child

The wide-ranging theories that comment on play describe many aspects of it; the process and outcomes of play, the child's actions in their world, making sense of their interactions with others and their surroundings. Some definitions of play focus on the simple mechanisms of play that humans share with other animals, others look at the complex cognitive processes involved, which appear to be most developed in humans. There are many varied views on play and to explore them all would take a book in itself; so we will focus on a few to explore different aspects in some depth. The chapter will end with a brief discussion of brain-based epistemology, a way of 'thinking about thinking' based on how the brain works (Edelman 2006).

Play is . . .

When preparing the definition of play used in this book – summarized as 'self-chosen, engaging and satisfying' – a critical comparison of others' views on play was prepared (see Appendix 1). Eighteen diverse views were contrasted and compared to try to expose the similarities and differences between the definitions. Some views were identical, others quite unique; some definitions described the process of playing, others included perceived benefits of play, what the originator felt it offered the child. Some described the physical functions of play, some considered the social or cultural aspects, others the imaginal and spiritual aspects of play.

In his seminal work *Homo Ludens* (1950), Johan Huizinga captured many significant characteristics of human play. He listed his key elements: 'All play is a voluntary activity; it is not "ordinary" or "real" life; it contains its own course and meaning; it creates order; it has a tendency to be beautiful; it promotes social groupings which are different from the common world' (1950: 8–12). Huizinga defined humans as 'playing people', yet in his final analysis stated, 'The human mind can only disengage itself from the magic circle of play by turning towards the ultimate. Logical thinking does not go far enough' (1950: 212). With that caution, let's see how far logic takes us.

Catherine Garvey (1977), in her influential definition that clearly borrows from Huizinga, said that play was spontaneous and voluntary, involved some active engagement on the part of the player, had certain systematic relations to what is not play, was pleasurable, enjoyable and had no extrinsic goals. Many of these elements are in the full list of *The Essential Characteristics of Playing* in Table 1.1. However Garvey, while hinting at their inclusion, did not include play as a process, or using the mind and body in a space that was sufficiently safe. Basing her views in part on Piaget's earlier work (1962), she tended to favour the cognitive benefits of play over other elements.

In contrast, Tina Bruce based three of her *Twelve Features of Play* (2001) on relationships such as playing alone, parallel with others, associatively, or cooperatively in pairs or groups, probably adding to Vygotsky's views of social development (1976). Bruce also included what she considered to be the outcomes of play – rehearsing the future and 'wallowing' in learning – emphasizing growth and educational outcomes.

It might be expected that an animal behaviourist like Marc Bekoff might offer a different perspective, but he felt that play was, 'The way in which human and nonhuman animals learn what's right and what's wrong' (Ip-Dip 74 2011). He also commented on the purpose of play that it was essential for young animals of all species and was perhaps the most important behaviour in which human and non-human animals engage. Bekoff looked at animal play and human play, and found similarities in physical play and social bonding activities.

Another animal behaviourist in accord with Garvey (1977), Gordon Burghardt (Ip-Dip 74 2011), also felt that play came from within the animal (it has an 'endogenous component'), and recognized that it takes place in a *relaxed field*; animals under threat, whether real or perceived, find it hard to play. And while for Burghardt play was about repeated performances, he felt that it offered limited immediate function. He also recognized the changed nature within the play exchange and said that it contained 'structural or temporal differences' – that, when playing, animals ignored or emphasized social structures (i.e. playing with bigger or smaller peers) and that time was less relevant when playing – in contrast to hunting when timing might be crucial. Burghardt takes play further back in the evolutionary spiral; he claims that rudimentary play forms are present in reptiles, fish and even insects.

The point about 'structural or temporal differences' was also considered important by Charalampos (known as Babis) Mainemelis and Sarah Ronson (2006) in their paper on play and creativity in organizational settings; they felt that play was about 'exploring boundaries in time and space'. Like Garvey, they stated that play created a positive feeling in the player and that outcomes were not considered important as there was a 'loose association between means and ends'. Yet Mainemelis and Ronson (2006) also recognized that play was about attraction to new experiences, be they to do with pretence or boundary testing; play helps transform the nature of an activity with the 'voluntary exercise of control systems' – playing with pretence and the potential for new forms or new ways of doing things; as Brian Eno put it, 'Let's see what would happen if the world was like this'. Mainemelis and Ronson comment on quite subtle dimensions of play that occur cognitively and emotionally in humans.

Stuart Lester and Wendy Russell recognize this other dimension of play in their paper written for the International Play Association (2010). They state how, rather than being about future benefits, play is of the moment, where children can change rules and roles, boundaries and borders, in order to, 'seek out uncertainty in order to triumph over it' (Lester and Russell 2010: x). They go on to challenge one of the most dominant paradigms to do with play: 'It is understandable to see children's play as a rehearsal for adult life, but there is little empirical evidence to support this' (Lester and Russell 2010: x).

As we can see, play has been described in many ways and with many attributes ascribed to it; how can we reconcile these various views?

Dominant paradigms

In the developed, western world – which has its roots in the Greek and Roman empires in Europe – the epitome of civilization is deemed to be rational, cognitive thinking, where issues are conceptualized and problems thought through symbolically or metaphorically. Many of the most valued institutions in the west, even if creative or belief based, have at heart a respect for the intellectual arguments used to make them credible. In the west, the *Enlightenment* in the seventeenth century led to a move away from the then current thinking grounded in tradition and faith. Instead of a power elite based on the Church and a belief in divine creation, the rational scientist came to the fore through the work of, for example, Isaac Newton, Benjamin Franklin, then later Darwin, Einstein and Crick, Watson, Wilkins and Rosalind Franklin, the people who identified the structure of DNA – the 'building blocks' of life itself.

For more than 300 years, science and mathematics have developed, searching for an objective truth in the nature of the world, supported by symbolic thinking and representation. Cultural and artistic systems went down a different but parallel path, again moving away from elements that sanctified or praised a divinity, to elements that represented reality with all its flaws. Yet cognitive and conceptual thinking holds the high ground in most fields dominant in the west; work with the hands and body has for many people been devalued and reduced to the actions of a machine – even if carried out by a human. And what started as an object-based trading system – economics – has become a purely symbolic domain, where electronic symbols determine the success of people, companies and nations.

In the continuing search for 'truth' in the twentieth century, we arrived at the concepts of post-modernism and post-structuralism, which in a very brief explanation, might be described as recognizing that all thinking and so all human structures cannot be fully understood by *Homo sapiens* as we cannot be objective about the subjective reality we are living in. We can strive for full understanding, but we can never truly know it; we tend to explain reality through difference – comparing experiences with phenomena they are like or unlike.

So, in summary, we have a variety of dominant paradigms that were formed at least 500 years ago in some cases:

- the religious belief – a divine force determines the nature of the universe and the fate of everything within it
- the scientific explanation – all things in the world may be described rationally by examining the objective facts of the universe, verifiable by observation and experiment
- the cognitive conviction – conceptual thinking is more developed than acting on instinct or perception, and is therefore more highly valued; often linked to formal education

- the economic point of view – everything has a value and the 'market' will determine that value

- the post-modernist perspective – context is everything and 'truth' can only be considered through a rigorous examination of language and relationships.

What Sutton-Smith called the developmental *rhetoric* (1997) runs through some of these views, the conviction that growth and change may be controlled, and that adulthood is the 'normal' condition of humankind. (*Rhetoric* is sometimes described as an unsupported argument, or belief.) Adam Phillips gave a good reply to that view and commented on a defining characteristic of play: 'There is no purpose to the child's life other than the pleasure of living it; it is not the child, in other words, who believes in something called development' (Phillips 1998: 21).

These paradigms each have their own views of play, some of which are more prevalent than others:

- the universe is at play, the god-given spirit of *lila* pervades everything
- evolution has caused certain types of behaviour to arise and play is one of those
- minds develop in structured ways, becoming more logical and rational as they leave playful things behind
- land and natural resources are commodities and must be developed to create a profit; children are attracted to the many versions of electronic play created by the market
- play is of the moment; an everyday phenomenon that changes according to context and intent
- play is a way of learning, a way of preparing for adulthood.

How can we make sense of these different views? Is any one view telling the *truth*? What does each have to offer? As Ken Wilber has said, 'Everybody is right; more specifically, everybody ... has some important pieces of truth' (2000). Using the Integral Play Framework, we can analyse and assess the views to see what they reveal about the world the adult/practitioner operates within, and therefore the connection to children's play, what they offer and what they might omit.

Using the Integral Play Framework to understand different views of play

As the Integral Play Framework describes the child's play world through four different filters, it may be used as a tool to examine various perspectives (see

Figure 3.1). For example, the ancient Roman saying, a 'healthy mind in a healthy body', focused on the individual, rather than the collective cultural and social worlds. But more recent writers, such as Piaget (1962), may be located within the mind quadrant. His focus on four stages of cognitive development – sensorimotor, preoperational, concrete operational and formal operational – describe an individual's emerging development from a world dominated by senses to a world of observation, and then a world of symbolic, abstract thinking. While the use of a body to accomplish these tasks was implied, Piaget's focus was on the work of the mind, though with an awareness of the interplay with 'our biological reality' (as reported by Kagen 1982: 42).

Vygotsky (1976) added to the cognitive dimension with the cultural one; he recognized that children interacted with others and that those others could offer support to the child. This was significant in that it showed the role of the adult or other in the child's life, and that cognitive development did not pass through some genetically defined stages but was evolving, based on experiences and interaction. Vygotsky acknowledged the use of the body in children's growth – he commented that 'all functions of consciousness . . . originally arise from action' (Vygotsky 1976: 539) – yet still his focus was on the child's mental development.

A theorist who commented on the physical aspects of play was Spencer (1904), augmenting Schiller's 'surplus energy' theory of play (1862) – that when animals had no need to find food or defend themselves from predators, they spent energy in 'aimless activity' such as play. Spencer argued that children had energy to use for play because their parents provided for their hunger and protection needs. This view of play looked at play as a bodily function, a mostly physical manifestation of the 'play impulse', as Schiller named it.

The social aspect of play was emphasized in Parten's 'Stages of Play' classification of children's play (1932). Parten observed American children (aged

	Internal	External
Individual	My mind	My body
Shared	Our cultural world	Our social world

Figure 3.1 The Integral Play Framework simplified.

2 to 5) and decided on six different types of play, the first of which was not really play:

1   unoccupied play – where the child is just observing what else is happening
2   solitary play – a child is alone and focused on the activity they are engaged in; often such children are unaware of what others are doing
3   onlooker play – children watch others at play but do not engage in it; they may engage in conversation about the play, without joining in the activity
4   parallel play – a child plays separately from others but close to them and does the same type of activity
5   associative play – children are interested in the people playing but not in the activity they are doing
6   cooperative play – children are interested in the others playing and in the activity they are doing; the activity may be organized, and participants often have assigned roles.

Parten's model emphasized the social dimensions of play. All stages of the model related to the presence or absence of others; she did not differentiate in the kinds of activity, just in the relationship of the players. Her argument was hierarchical in that she stated that as children became older, developed better communication skills and were able to interact more with peers, the solitary and parallel types of play grew less frequent, and the social (associative and cooperative) types of play became more usual.

In addition to describing humans as 'playing people', Huizinga is known for his statement that 'Culture arises in the form of play'; he saw that 'Competitions and exhibitions as amusements do not proceed from culture, they rather precede it' (1950: 46–47). While he commented on many aspects of play, Huizinga recognized that play and culture were inseparable – the characteristics and rules of play were to be found everywhere in culture.

The aspect of culture was also described by Roger Caillois (1961: 36) in his categorization of play as *ludus*; a controlling principle that constrains the natural 'playfulness' of play (what he termed *paidia*). Caillois claimed that *ludus* created a culturally appropriate outlet to normalize and define play. For example, the playful impulse to mimic others and wear costumes is made culturally relevant through theatre and ritual; simple games of chance like counting games or dice-based games become complex gambling activities. These two categories define a continuum between fully playful activities and culturally appropriate play or games, between *paidia* and *ludus*, or from childish activities to more formal ones. Caillois also named four forms of play, using Greek terms to identify them, as follows.

1   *Mimesis* is mimicry, make-believe and play-acting; actions that involve imagination and interaction with others, and that become theatre and dramatic spectacle as the rules and structure increase.

2   *Agon* is competitive play with strong social and physical aspects, where humans would be pitted against one another in order to find out who was strongest or fastest. The playful activities would be informal running about (tag) and wrestling (rough and tumble play); the more formal being sports contests and games. Sutton-Smith (1997) later called this form of play the 'Play as Power' rhetoric.

3   *Alea* describes games of chance such as *Eeeny Meeny Miney Mo*, or simple dice games (Snakes and Ladders), but also embraced formal gambling using devices (roulette, dice) or unpredictable outcomes (betting). This 'Play as Fate' rhetoric (Sutton-Smith 1997) involves a sense of magical reality in the simpler games – 'fate decides' – or a false sense of objective predictability, based on logic and/or experience.

4   *Ilinx* is the type of play that creates a temporary disruption of perception, as with vertigo, dizziness or disorienting changes in direction of movement. This becomes culturally acceptable through, for example, playground roundabouts, funfair rides, amusement park rides, skiing and mountain climbing. Ilinx is a physical form of play where the body is put through experiences to create excessive stimulus through the senses of sight, touch, balance and acceleration.

Caillois focused on the physical, social and cultural aspects of play, with truly imaginative, cognitive or problem-solving play not described within his system.

With some similarity to Caillois, Brian Sutton-Smith devised expressions to describe the different manifestations of play, what he called *rhetorics*: 'The word rhetoric is used here in its modern sense, as being a persuasive discourse, or an implicit narrative, wittingly or unwittingly adopted by members of a particular affiliation to persuade others of the variety and worthwhileness of their beliefs' (Sutton-Smith 1997: 8).

As well as the *rhetorics* already mentioned, Sutton-Smith (1997) has described seven in total, as follows.

1   Play as Progress – the dominant view in the twentieth century, play's purpose was seen to contribute to cognitive growth, and/or the development of moral standards acceptable to others.

2   Play as Fate – play is an aspect of destiny, whether 'magical' as in dice games (as described above) and determined by cultural beliefs, or 'atomic cause and effect' (the 'butterfly effect' – where large-scale actions are determined by very small changes elsewhere in the world), i.e. dominated by aspects in the physical world.

3   Play as Power – play is a representation of conflict, usually through sports contests and athletic activities, that builds up the status of those involved or who control it (*agon*, as described by Caillois); located in the external half of the Integral Play Framework, using bodily power to dominate socially.

4   Play as Identity – play that confirms, maintains or advances the identity and so control of the community of players, i.e. those in the game, who know the cultural boundaries of the world created.

5   Play as the Imaginary – usually applied to playful improvisation leading to flexibility and creativity in many forms; again located in the internal, subjective domain of the model, but this time recognizing the intrinsic nature of play, how it can take place without any obvious external trigger.

6   Play as Exploration of the Self – where play is applied by the individual to challenging and risky activity that explores the human condition, whether for fun, relaxation or escape from other pressures; this activity could be mental and so internal or physical and so tested 'in the world'.

7   Play as Frivolous – play that is 'anti-work', ironic and foolish, but in the slapstick way of Laurel and Hardy, and the knowing way of jesters and fools, who historically were the only ones able to poke fun at royalty. This rhetoric is active in the social quadrant of the Framework where it is 'beneath' and 'beyond' social structures considered normal; actions seen as 'silly' – *we don't do that here* – or serious – *what you are doing challenges my view of the world* – according to intent.

These descriptions cover all quadrants of the Integral Play Framework and show how varied forms of play are valued by people with diverse interests. For example, people who believe in play as progress are unlikely to value frivolous play; those who prefer hard work and physical challenges are unlikely to be satisfied with games of chance; those who play alone, may not like team games or group activities and so on. The Framework helps explain those activities that are mostly physical and carried out in the environment, or those mostly carried out in the mind and imagination; it also helps make clear the elements that are mainly individual or group activities.

Making sense of play types

Names have been given to different forms of play ever since people have been describing playful activities. Plato (428–347 BCE) wrote about what we now call the physiological benefits of play – how play involving movement (or locomotion) is good for our bodies; Groos (1861–1946) wrote about how role-play prepared children for adulthood; Steiner (1861–1925) believed in creative play, and so on. In 1996, after reading through the various views on play, Bob Hughes published *A playworker's taxonomy of play types*. Originally containing just 15 play types, the list was updated in 2002 to make 16 (a brief description of the terms Hughes used in given in Appendix 2).

Hughes recognized that such lists are subjective and influenced by the compiler's views when he described it as 'A taxonomy' rather than '*The* taxonomy'. The categorization of play types was intended to help adults describe the different types of behaviour they saw when children were playing; not all play involves the same set of activities or affects, so having clear descriptions of the different types aids adults in saying what they think is happening when children are playing. Hughes' aim was to rationalize different forms of play into clear categories – for example, running, jumping, walking, climbing were all seen as using the large muscles of the body to move about and so were defined as locomotor play. There are other ways to categorize play – for example, Sutton-Smith (1997: 4–5) has identified more than 300 different types of play for children and adults. And early years practitioners may be more familiar with *schemas* or patterns of linked behaviour; these are discussed more fully below. Having a smaller rather than a large list helps with remembering the definitions so that they may be applied in work with children.

To help explain how forms of play may manifest at different times and degrees of maturity or understanding, the play types (Hughes 1996a, 2002) have been mapped on to the Integral Play Framework (see Figure 3.2). This list of play types may be familiar to UK play practitioners working with children aged 5–16 years but is used here as the terms describing the activity are mostly in clear English; e.g. creativity play, role play, exploratory play. One exception that may need clarifying is deep play, which Hughes describes as 'risky or even potentially life threatening experiences' – other writers (Ackerman, Bruce) use the term to mean involving or immersive play.

The framework uses the 16 play types described by Hughes (2002) and adds in another 11 play types suggested by the Integral Play Framework model; the text in brackets [ ] shows types of play not in Hughes' taxonomy yet suggested by other authors and practical experience with children (see Appendix 2 for details). The additions to Hughes' list are to broaden it to include play types exhibited by very young children (perceptual play and impulsive play), to separate out different forms of play (e.g. creative cognitive play and creative artistic play) or to include play types omitted in the original list (e.g. family play and sexual play).

The framework shows that different play forms are dominant in the four quadrants of the model; locomotor play, rough and tumble play and sexual play are primarily (though not exclusively) about using the body; communication and social play are about getting on with others. It therefore suggests that the different forms of play help us understand the different aspects of

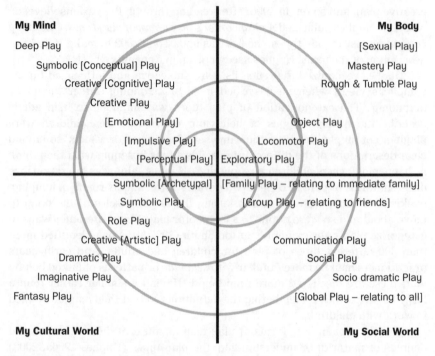

My Mind

Deep Play

Symbolic [Conceptual] Play

Creative [Cognitive] Play

Creative Play

[Emotional Play]

[Impulsive Play]

[Perceptual Play]

My Body

[Sexual Play]

Mastery Play

Rough & Tumble Play

Object Play

Locomotor Play

Exploratory Play

Symbolic [Archetypal]

Symbolic Play

Role Play

Creative [Artistic] Play

Dramatic Play

Imaginative Play

Fantasy Play

[Family Play – relating to immediate family]

[Group Play – relating to friends]

Communication Play

Social Play

Socio dramatic Play

[Global Play – relating to all]

My Cultural World

My Social World

Figure 3.2 The Integral Play Framework and play types.

Source: after Hughes (1996a), (2002).

being human – emotionally, physically, socially, culturally, cognitively and spiritually.

As Hughes recognized (2006: 5), play types may have evolved for distinct purposes – skill at running and jumping serves a separate purpose to getting on with others or making sounds – and there are likely to be different levels of ability within play types or with combinations of play types. For example, locomotor play, movement in all directions, will be different for a toddler and a teenager; and children may be socializing while running around. Recapitulative play, a recap of aspects of collective human evolutionary history, includes elements of all four quadrants – e.g. actions, feelings, rituals, roles – however it is likely that play forms evolved and emerged at varied times.

Hughes has speculated (2006) that types of play may vary from proto-types to mature types, or manifest to latent; that play types are not all of one 'level' and that mastery of any play type will evolve over time. Just so with types of play across species; the play face and the play bow are easy to spot when dogs are playing, and similar energies are visible in young humans. Yet, as humans mature, the signs and signals become more subtle and may be apparent only to family members or members of a clique – gang members take it a stage further and create signals, tags and language known only to the gang.

Overall the model helps us appreciate that different types of play evolved to contribute to children's life experiences and development; for children to miss out an aspect of their play may affect what they do, how they grow and how they behave later in life. For example, children who have had limited locomotor play, may be unfit or overweight; they may not feel comfortable during rough and tumble play, so may become isolated or feel 'picked on' – overweight children are less likely to take part in activities later in life that require active movement, such as dance, sports, cycling or jogging (Cassidy *et al.* 2010). Similarly, children who have not had a positive experience of family play may find it more difficult to get on with others through communication play or social play; they are less likely to see others as friendly or supportive, and may even be hostile towards them. And, as discussed earlier, children who do not play much in their early years are more likely to have smaller and less flexible brain structures.

Words of caution

Play types should never be used as a curriculum tool – they do not predict behaviour, they only describe it, for play is always a process, a way of doing something and not a particular activity. As Sylva and colleagues (1976: 244) stated, 'The essence of play is in the dominance of means over ends . . . in play the process is more important than the product'. Playing is therefore a way of being, a way of performing an activity rather than the activity itself; 'dressing-up' can be a functional activity of wearing a uniform, or it can be a playful expression of feeling or role. The difference is in the manner or mode of the player.

A daughter and her father were exiting from a building that was fitted with an electronic roller blind. While the girl was playfully 'limbo-ing' under the ascending roller, her father made a point of waiting until it had risen to his full 2m height. As he emerged, he smiled knowingly at his daughter. She ran ahead, and came to a series of street bollards that she proceeded to weave in-between, swaying slightly and raising her hands like a plane. When she came to the end of the row of bollards, she turned to her father and said, 'Ta-daa' and curtseyed slightly.

The play types only describe what the adult sees in a given moment, not what the child intended – children do not label play, adults do. A well-meaning adult could set up a table with artistic materials expecting that the children will participate in creative artistic play, yet the children could just as easily play rough and tumble or social play, or use the material as weapons in a mock snowball fight. If the adult recognizes that play should be chosen by the child they will understand this activity; on the other hand if the adult expects a certain outcome from the play, they may find the changes distracting or even disruptive to the setting plan. This will be discussed in more detail in Chapter 4.

Similarly, not every form of behaviour displayed by children can be described as playful. The formula 'c+e+s' aims to show that play activities should be chosen (c), engaging (e) and satisfying (s) for all players. The form of rough and tumble play known as hazing (or stag nights) – rituals or other activities using harassment or humiliation as a way of initiating a person into a group – may be playful for the people carrying it out but no fun at all (until the end, perhaps) for the hazing victim. When the victim understands the purpose of the activity, they may choose to 'play the game' and be satisfied that the activity has brought them closer to their friends, though there are cases on record of hazing going too far and victims being seriously hurt or killed. Behaviour more usually witnessed by adults might include a heated argument between two children; is that communication play or just an argument? A full-on argument is not likely to be satisfying at the time it occurs – too much emotion will be apparent; the play face is likely to be absent. However, if the argument is between two children who know each other well, it can drift between being play, playful and then not play. Two friends might pretend to be arguing, let's say about which TV programme is best. As the argument develops, one might go a little too far and imply that the other's parents are a little impoverished because they do not have the latest TV package. The one slighted then feels not so playful and may start hurling back quite venomous statements. The provocateur, realizing the crossing of boundaries, could choose to self-limit and agree with the statements that they are half-human and, to demonstrate, sticks out a tongue and starts swinging their arms like a monkey. The victim, recognizing the silliness of the situation, breaks into a smile and joins in the arm swinging and they go off hooting together.

Making sense of schemas

Another extensive categorization of play behaviours is with the use of *schema*, which were first popularized in child development theory by Piaget, who 'described sets of actions, as applied to situations, whether these were physical or mental, as schemas' (Langston and Abbot, in Bruce 2006: 99). Athey, who added extensively to the original idea, said they were 'patterns of repeatable behaviour into which experiences are assimilated and that are gradually co-ordinated ... Co-ordinations lead to higher-level and more powerful schemas' (Athey 1990: 37). Like play types, schemas describe the behaviour that adults see when children are playing, and simple schema combine to make complex schemas; Athey has said the process becomes more and more complex as children grow older until the overlapping becomes too difficult to identify the separate schema accurately.

Linked to Piaget's work, Athey identified four stages that children go through in exploring and using schema:

1   sensorimotor level – where physical action is carried out for its own sake

2   symbolic level – where objects are used to represent something else

3   functional dependency level – the child understands the relationship between two separate things

4   abstract thought level – where the schemas are used to support thought.

Other than stage one, these levels are mainly cognitive; a point emphasized by Worthington and Carruthers (2006: 148), who say that, 'most schemas are mathematical: for example *rotation, vertical* and *horizontal* schemas'. This seems an overly prescriptive view, which illustrates again that writers often describe models in terms of their own interests; if young children could be asked, it is unlikely that they would agree with that viewpoint. Many of the identified schemas make extensive use of the child's body, other objects and spaces, especially during the first three phases.

Athey believes that children explore different schemas in varied ways as they grow older; examples of the more common schemas include:

*   containment – putting materials inside an object that is capable of containing them

*   crossing a boundary – causing oneself, material or an object to go through a boundary and emerge at the other side

*   enclosure – enclosing oneself, an object or space

*   envelopment – covering or surrounding oneself, an object or space

*   rotation – turning, twisting or rolling oneself or objects in the environment around

*   trajectory – moving in or representing straight lines, arcs or curves

*   transporting – carrying objects or being carried from one place to another.

While schemas describe behaviour that is observable in children, in some settings it is believed that 'schema spotting' provides an analytical tool to the child's development. As in the discussion on play types, this appears to be an attempt to be desperately objective about what is in reality a varied and chaotic activity, namely playing. While children undoubtedly explore themes in their play, it is difficult to see this as an explicitly cognitive function; children are playing and wanting to see 'what if'.

In practice, the time differences between the four stages suggest that the process of change is more evolutionary and emergent than cognitive. Take, for example, the schema of rotation (which by itself could be considered to be *Ilinx* or vertigo according to Caillois' description, at the sensorimotor level the child might be twirling round and around. Stage 2 would be when the twirling is used to represent or symbolize a roundabout (symbolic play); when the child notices the connection between the speed of a wheel or a spinning top, and the time or distance it travels, would be characterized as functional dependence or Stage 3 (mastery play). Later when the child puts all of these ideas into words and expresses the logic behind rotation would be the fully cognitive Stage 4 (symbolic conceptual play). It is unlikely that these events would occur during a single year of a child's life or during a child's stay in one particular setting. By providing space and materials for children's self-directed exploration and play in the world, and for interaction with others in that space, adults would be able to provide for their experience and development, without needing to fit them into one theme or another.

Play has no defined start – or end

One model of play that recognizes the transformative potential of play is that proposed by Gordon and Esbjorn-Hargens (2007). They link play forms to the evolution of consciousness, with human developmental stages, in what they term the 'Eight Play Selves'. The model suggests how play changes according to the knowledge and awareness of the player. These Play Selves start with egocentric levels of awareness, becoming ethnocentric and then global in their awareness (see Table 3.1).

While these play selves are human-centred, they are connected to the wider cosmos at both ends of the continuum; Magical Players believe in superstition, charms and rituals, that wishing a thing makes it so; Unitive Players feel connected to everything. Unitive Play is universal play aligned with the concept of *lila* – the spirit of playfulness in everything; the concept that the universe is 'simply' the play of the gods.

However, as previously stated, play is apparent in 'simpler' forms with other animals – such play forms would not be described as 'Magical Play', but may be described as social play, locomotor play or rough and tumble play. Whether play stops with humans or extends into the world, the solar system or the galaxy is beyond the scope of this chapter, but evolution shows us that these traits started somewhere and do not necessarily end with the latest manifestation of consciousness. Play becomes more complex and all-encompassing as the players evolve. As Gordon and Esbjorn-Hargens state,

Table 3.1 The 'Eight Play Selves'.

Play Selves	Style of play	Examples
Magical Player	**Play as connection to cosmos** Balancing good and evil	Players have a strong desire for creating safety and satisfying their basic needs. Their play is often repetitious as they feel confused and anxious about the complexity of the world.
Aggressive Player	**Play as conquest** Acts of heroism	Play as conquest, the world for them is full of danger, with challenges around every corner. The players are in competition with others, and their play takes the form of acts of heroism, war games, 'chicken', drinking games, fighting.
Ordered Player	**Play as structure** Following the rules	Players define themselves through others, often with conformist personalities, abiding by the rules, and see play as structure. They suppress negative feelings and overemphasize positive ones.
Status Player	**Play as competition** Winning and losing	Players have greater independence and confidence, they emphasize rationality. They are drawn to achievement by being concise, efficient and effective. The world is experienced as predictable and measurable.
Sensitive Player	**Play as cooperation** Connecting and sharing	The individualistic player who emphasizes interpersonal connections by sharing experiences and acknowledging the contextual aspects of play (e.g. gender, class, race). They value feelings and express them, and understand their world is filled with diverse perspectives and competing truth claims.
Complex Player	**Play as chaos** Fast and unpredictable	Players are autonomous and welcome chaos and multiple variables; they understand the self as embedded in many contexts and dimensions. They tolerate others in spite of their negative traits and differences of opinions or values, and experience their world as multi-dimensional with overlapping contexts and systems.
Dynamic Player	**Play as transformative** Multi-modal and multi-dimensional	The player who integrates multi-modal and multi-dimensional elements across contexts in service of humanity. Aware of the subtle ways the ego filters experience, they recognize paradox and understand others in developmental terms, and encounter them without judgement. They experience the world as a place full of potential and paradox.
Unitive Player	**Play as lila** Spontaneous, highly creative, original and open	The Unitive Player is free of the constraints of any limited identity, and able to be spontaneous and open under any circumstance. They view others as manifestations of Being and experience the world as an immanent expression of timeless Spirit. (Much of what is understood about this stage is based on inferences suggested by the other stages.)

Source: Gordon and Esbjorn-Hargens (2007).

'The play forms of more developed stages are almost unintelligible to those of less developed stages' (2007: 218). An Aggressive Player would not understand the 'fairness' or self-limiting behaviour of a Sensitive Player; an Ordered Player may find the unpredictability of the Complex Player unnerving. This is significant as some children will find pleasure in 'simply playing' by running around, others may be having 'peak experiences' with play at all levels and forms, including those forms considered transformative or transcendental, yet it may take half a lifetime to become familiar and comfortable with some of the evolved forms of play. Of this journey, Gordon and Esbjorn-Hargens have this to say:

> Play also provides a way of exploring the developmental edges of players' body, mind, and spirit in a way that enables the players to put boundaries around what they are willing to risk ... Play engenders the optimism needed to take risks and shows that taking risks can bring rewards.
>
> *(2007: 217)*

Play offers a way for players to 'be in control of being out of control' (Gordon and Esbjorn-Hargens 2007: 216); the boundaries of behaviour and experience are defined by the play and the confidence and knowledge levels of the player. Once the risk has been taken and the boundary crossed, the player can reflect, looking back at their previous play, and realize that what was once considered 'impossible' is now an everyday occurrence. Applying this concept to the Integral Play Framework, it describes when mastery is gained over a particular condition such as riding a bike, and the rider understands what was not 'do-able' before, or when playing with a mixed group of children, whereas previously the player might have felt threatened or uncomfortable with such a group.

> To say that play is essential to the human species is to corroborate what creative scientists, artists, and the great saints have understood as central to their own activities. Play, fantasy, the imagination, and free exploration of possibilities: these are the central powers of the human person.
>
> *Brian Swimme (1984: 64)*

The *Eight Play Selves* offers a model that encompasses elements of Piaget's stages and extends them into adult play; as with all models what it excludes is just as significant as what it includes in the search for the true nature of play.

Regarding the 'truth' of human consciousness and experience

Truth is a shifting concept and what was once thought to be solely the jurisdiction of the gods, is now debated intensely by humans. Thinkers in the twentieth century (e.g. Heidegger, Sartre, Merleau-Ponty, Derrida) taught us that truth is dependent on the context under which it is discussed. However, starting from physics and evolutionary biology, with recognition of psychological concepts, Gerald Edelman has established what he calls a *brain-based epistemology*, a way of 'thinking about thinking' built on how the brain works (Edelman 2006). Using his wide-ranging knowledge of the brain's structures, and following extensive research from a variety of sources, Edelman shows that, while the brain has several distinct regions, it does not hold consciousness in any one area; as he states, 'Consciousness is not a thing, it is a process' (Edelman 2006: 41).

The separate parts of the brain contribute to consciousness with the emotional elements prompting responses which are then made sense of by the 'higher' cerebral cortex, though the conscious element also has a role to play in making distinctions about what is valued by the individual: 'Interactions among core systems, non-conscious memory systems, and signals from value systems operate together to account for the richness of human behaviour' (Edelman 2006: 39). The complexity and richness of this process, evolving and emerging in each individual, means that no two brains are identical, even those of identical twins (Edelman 2006: 55); 'The main point is that truth is not a given, it is a value that must be worked for during our personal and interpersonal interactions' (Edelman 2006: 150).

Edelman argues that our consciousness, sense of self and therefore our 'truth' emerges and is formed by our interaction with the world. This quality was formed as our ancestors strove for continued existence, for 'The econiche in which animals must survive has an enormous number of signals to which an individual must adapt' (Edelman 2006: 102). In the modern world our brains still need these signals in order to adapt well to our world; there is a danger that as environments are increasingly controlled and 'made safe' for humans (especially in the industrialized world), that richness and diversity is lost and so is our ability to develop and adapt.

It is the interplay between our environment and our thoughts that creates who we are; our bodies exist in nature, in the world, and cannot be removed from that world. Yet in our heads we have experiences of the world that 'feel natural' or 'are second nature' even when scientific evidence tries to convince us otherwise. Edelman makes the case that, 'The brain-based approach ... provides scientific grounds for a pluralistic view of truth ... accepting empirical data from neuroscience as well as psychology to buttress our views of the origin and nature of human knowledge' (2006: 148). Artists and rationalists argue for the experience of existence; scientists and reductionists would claim that everything can be explained by collecting and sorting data to arrive at facts about the world. The truth appears to be that our lived experience is a combination of both; we are shaped by the environment in which we grow and exist, yet we also make decisions about our experiences which affect our value system, and how we think in and about that world.

An example of this system in action is that the brain does not need a 'language acquisition device' as originally proposed by Chomsky (1965). The variety of languages around the world shows that every human being has the capacity to develop a language; yet each human being taken at birth to a different culture would learn the speech of that culture.

> Language acquisition is epigenetic . . . We do not inherit a language of thought. Instead, concepts are developed from the brain's mapping of its own perceptual maps. Ultimately therefore, concepts are initially about the world.
>
> *Gerald Edelman (2006: 153–154)*

This is quite exciting in that it is their sense and experiences of the world that allow children's language and thoughts and cognition to emerge – and the process is led by the individual. Clearly while others in the environment may have an influence on that experience, the process is innate; while it may be helped or hampered by intervention, it cannot be shaped without a willingness to engage and acceptance on the part of the child.

The brain and therefore consciousness is not shaped simply by the genetic material we inherit from our parents; the development of consciousness is a selectional system influenced by the phenomena of our existence. This system allows enormous combinatorial freedom for thought and imagery; this helps us understand, 'The complexity, the irreversibility, and the historical contingency of our phenomenal experience' (Edelman 2006: 143). We are each unique individuals shaped by our genetic material and also by the experiences we have in our lives. And the good news is that the process continues throughout our lives. While there are 'sensitive periods' in early growth and adolescence, the brain continues to build connections throughout life. As these patterns are not fixed by a genetic pattern, the patterns may also reform following illness or trauma, as has been shown in extreme cases of brain injury where previously inactive parts of the brain can 'wake up' to help make up for the lost function elsewhere.

Edelman's brain-based epistemology rejects the notion that 'art, aesthetics, and ethics can be reduced to a series of epigenetic rules of brain action . . . no divorce is necessary between science and the humanities' (2006: 156). This is an excellent summary of the unique nature of human existence, and explains how the four-quadrant Integral Play Framework helps map the varied experiences of children and, ultimately, human beings.

Questions to help practitioners make sense of other views

- What is the dominant paradigm (concept or theory) in the setting you work in? Do you agree with that paradigm? What do you think it offers when working with children; what do you think is missing?
- Many models were influenced by Piaget's 'ages and stages' mode of thinking – do you think this still a relevant way to look at children? What do you think is true about what Piaget says, and what do you think other models offer that is better?
- Can you apply the Integral Play Framework to the models you use in your thinking about play? Does your model have both internal (subjective) and external (objective) dimensions? Does your model aim to be holistic? Does it describe different levels of human experience?

4

Supporting provision for children's playing

Children can play anywhere so why do adults feel the need to offer provision for play? The many ways to support playing children at home, in the neighbourhood, in special places and the wider environment will be discussed in this chapter. However, we will do it with a caution about the things to be aware of when helping sustain play opportunities. Approaches to good practice will be considered, from working with children to working with policy and governments to advocate for play.

Any environment can support play, however the more the environment is stimulating enough to invite play, the more play is likely to take place. Such an environment must be sufficiently non-threatening for the child to feel comfortable in that space, and ideally it should stimulate enthusiasm in the player – to be enthused is to be 'possessed by divine spirit' – some would say an essential of true play!

The environment should offer sufficient stimulus for the play to continue. In many 'boring' playgrounds, it may be the fact of the space itself is enough for play to proceed (as we believe play begins as a desire within the child that is made manifest in behaviour in the world); e.g. the child may run around rather than being cooped up in a small space. However, in good environments for play, opportunities and affordances (Gibson 1977) are all around, waiting to be found or for players to notice. According to the age, ability, understanding and experience of the child, some opportunities and affordances may be too high, too low, too closed, too open, too safe, too risky, until like Goldilocks they find one that is 'just right'.

Why do adults feel the need to offer provision for play?

In many parts of the world, there is not a need to make provision for play as children are able to play in their communities and in nature. They might get moved on from time to time, and some places such as temples and churches are considered off limits, but many places are play spaces as the adults accept children in their society. In the west adults have felt the need to offer recreation places in towns and cities to compensate for the loss of green space close to where they live.

Recreation spaces emerged in the UK in the middle of the nineteenth century, in part influenced by the ideas of writer John Ruskin, who felt that town folk needed spaces to 'recreate' as compensation for the energy expended during the working week. The first recreation ground in the USA was built in 1887. A comment made more than 100 years ago on the need for playgrounds for children has as much relevance today as when it was written:

> City streets are unsatisfactory playgrounds for children because of the danger, because most good games are against the law, because they are too hot in summer, and because in crowded sections of the city they are apt to be schools of crime. Neither do small back yards nor ornamental grass plots meet the needs of any but the very small children. Older children who would play vigorous games must have places especially set aside for them; and, since play is a fundamental need, playgrounds should be provided for every child as much as schools. This means that they must be distributed over the cities in such a way as to be within walking distance of every boy and girl, as most children cannot afford to pay carfare.
>
> *President Theodore Roosevelt (1907: 1163)*

The early playgrounds would often have metal and timber structures for children to climb, swing and balance on; the planning and format of them changed little until the middle of the twentieth century. These play spaces would be what most people would recognize as play provision in many countries, the town and park playgrounds with space for run-around play or with dedicated equipment for children to play on and with. The emphasis on these playgrounds was with physical movement and a wish to help children discover how to move and balance well.

In 1953 Lady Allen of Hurtwood was inspired to bring the concept of the self-build, or 'junk', playground from Denmark to the UK. Later known as adventure playgrounds, these spaces rapidly developed mostly in London but also through the UK and then other countries throughout the world. Adventure playgrounds became sanctuaries for children to play freely, running around, climbing, making friends, yet with an adult close by who understood their needs and could help when necessary. They were messy places for children to make things as the fancy took them; models, masks, costumes, dens, supported by an adult, a playwork practitioner who helped with material, prompts and tools. Adventure playgrounds were spaces for children to play in relative safety, challenging themselves and those around them and cared for by adults sensitive to their needs; overall they were not just spaces with equipment, they were places of community and communion for the children and the adults who chose to work with them.

More recently, public play spaces have been designed to meet adult agendas such as keeping fit and reducing obesity, offering maths and problem-solving opportunities, using bright primary colours in manufacture, because it was believed 'those are the colours that stimulate children'. While there is still considerable evidence of these elements in modern playgrounds, there has been a return to gross physical play and natural elements.

Ideas from the design of adventure playgrounds have found their way into recreation playgrounds so that, in the early twenty-first century, more children's playgrounds have timber structures (rather than metal ones), netting frames and bridges, dens, sand pits and water features, and are built with an awareness of the topography or landscape on which the playground is built. The purpose of these playgrounds was to offer children more control in how and what they played with, and with awareness that children needed quiet spaces to socialize as well as large spaces to run around.

These concepts have been further extended into the idea of the 'natural playground' that uses elements such as trees and bushes, small hills and valleys, textured pathways and 'natural' water features alongside boulders, other rock structures or sculptures and environmental art. Research by Moore (1986) has shown that formal playgrounds need to be balanced with marginal areas that appear to be spare or waste ground, ideally a wooded area or field, but that to children are areas they can claim for themselves. In recent times these areas have been renamed 'slack spaces' – the bits of ground that no one except children knows how to use (CABE 2004). The idea of playing outdoors in industrialized countries seems to have come full circle in a growing desire by some adults to return to nature and 'freely roaming' children (Wild Network 2013).

There is a strong rationale for play provision rooted in the perceived benefits of good play opportunities for children. This rationale is supported by some government policies affecting children including those of the United Nations and national movements. The United Nations Convention on the Rights of the Child Article 31 sets the international standard for the need for play:

1   Every child has the right to rest and leisure, to engage in play and recrea-
    tional activities appropriate to the age of the child and to participate
    freely in cultural life and the arts.
2   Member governments shall respect and promote the right of the child to
    participate fully in cultural and artistic life and shall encourage the provi-
    sion of appropriate and equal opportunities for cultural, artistic, recrea-
    tional and leisure activity.

In 2013, in a review of implementation of the rights of the child under the Convention on the Rights of the Child, concern was expressed about the poor recognition given by states to Article 31 (Lansdown 2013). In a restatement of the value of the Article, the following points (among others) were emphasized.

- Play and recreation are essential to the health and well-being of children, and promote the development of creativity, imagination, self-confidence, self-efficacy, and physical, social cognitive and emotional strength and skills.
- Both play and recreation can take place when children are on their own, together with their peers, or with supportive adults.
- Involvement in a community's cultural life is an important element of children's sense of belonging.
- In addition, children reproduce, transform, create and transmit culture through, for example, their imaginative play, songs, dance, animation, stories, painting, games, street theatre, puppetry, festivals, etc.
- Finally, rest and leisure are as important to children's development as the basics of nutrition, housing, health care and education.

Adults will provide play opportunities to help meet the needs they perceive in children's lives – the need to make choices, the need to be physically active, the need to socialize. Increasingly in the west, parents have felt the need to take children to settings where the activities offered, whether sport, dance, drama or extra scholastic study, help their children towards a specific path for future success. In the market-led sector prevalent in the west, settings were meeting parents' needs by offering programmes that satisfy these demands. As Gray (2013: 273) put it, 'Kids are more likely to engage in formal adult-directed sports than in pickup games, more likely to take karate classes than have snowball wars with other kids'. Fortunately there are lots of types of space out there for children to play in.

Different types of play space

There are many different forms of play space in the modern world, but for clarity we will look at just three types: designated play spaces where adults work in support of the play; designated play spaces with adults who may supervise the space but not the play; and all other spaces where children can play, and adults are not usually present (see Table 4.1 – these descriptions should be read as generic; there will be exceptions in every case). The role of adults in the play space will be discussed more in the next chapter.

Some play spaces have adults (often called playworkers or playwork practitioners) who support or facilitate play with children. While the role of

Table 4.1 Types of play space – with or without adults and formal provision.

	Lots of formal provision	Some formal provision	No or limited formal provision
Designated play spaces – adults in support of the play	Adventure playgrounds Indoor play centres Holiday playschemes Inclusive play projects	Out-of-school clubs Residential holidays Hospital play	Play rangers Play buses, mobile play provision
Designated play spaces – adults may supervise the space but not the play	Public playgrounds, play parks, recreation spaces Amusement parks, destination venues	Schools, forest schools Public houses, supermarkets Housing estates, city centres Home	Games pitches, playing fields
All other spaces where children can play – adults not usually present			Wild places, woods, fields, beaches Marginal or 'slack' spaces, streets, cemeteries, disused factories, etc. Anywhere

these adults will be discussed in the next chapter, note that the provision ranges from sites with lots of formal play equipment such as adventure playgrounds, play-centres and play projects, to sites with no formal equipment but the active support of an adult. Examples of these sites include play buses and mobile play provision (with the play offer usually supplied from a vehicle), or with the relatively new role of play rangers – adults who facilitate play with little equipment or only what is freely available in the environment. Sites with adults supporting play but with reduced formal accommodation for play include out-of-school clubs and residential holidays, where adults may work in or adapt an environment to make it more suitable for play, or hospital practitioners who use play to help children cope with or pass through hospital more easily.

The traditional playground would fall into the middle category; designated play spaces with no playworkers present, though there may be other adults in control of the space. Traditional playgrounds made available for community use are usually available free of charge, and are often located in public parks or recreation areas. The first 'amusement park' in the UK was established at Wicksteed Park in 1921, and is still run according to the founder's principles; it claims to be the largest free playground in Europe. The idea of the amusement park has been copied since then and has developed into destination venues that have moved away from purely play experiences into thrill and entertainment activity, such as that found at Alton Towers and Blackpool Pleasure Beach in the UK, and the Disney and Universal Studio theme parks in the USA and elsewhere.

Other designated spaces include places where play opportunities are offered such as in schools, next to public houses and supermarkets, on housing estates and in the home or garden. Possibilities for play will vary, though will usually include a variation on climbing, swinging or sliding equipment; they will not include the full range of possible experiences that are found in more formal provision. Increasingly, too, many city centres in Europe and the USA are setting aside space for community recreation, sometimes including water fountains and other play experiences. Games pitches and playing fields will not have formal play equipment but are made available for organized games and may be used for informal play when not used for other purposes.

Finally, almost any other space in the environment, even if actively hostile, will be a potential space for play. Children do not need provision to be made available to them, a moment of play can occur anywhere and, as Moore (1986) said, children will claim 'empty' spaces to make their own away from adult gaze and control. Natural places such as beaches and woods are useful, but for city dwellers, so are quiet streets, empty buildings such as old factories and warehouses, and even cemeteries.

If children will play anywhere, then why does provision need to be made available for them to play, and what is it that adults add to the mix? What is wrong with providing space for play and what is wrong with not making provision available?

Things to be aware of when supporting provision for play

Players must feel safe in the environment in which they play. While there are exceptions to this rule, generally the environment should offer sufficient physical and psychological safety for the player (Else, after Rogers 1961). Many children in the UK in the twenty-first century would not play well where there are large gaping holes in the floor or where equipment is poorly maintained and in danger of falling down. Likewise they may not play well in spaces where there are bullies, or people telling them what to do or how to behave. However, we do see children across the world who will play in these conditions, through necessity or lack of an alternative; children who live in industrial areas, run-down areas, war-torn areas. In such environments, the children adapt to and accommodate the risks, adjusting their play accordingly. Some people would prefer to eliminate such forms of play from children's lives, yet they play because they must, and so take pleasure, learn skills and take risks in those environments that others less used to the conditions would not be able to do.

A vital element of feeling comfortable in the environment is when the individual feels an acceptance of the environment – there is sufficient space that the child can claim it as their own – and external evaluation is absent, whether through rules, standards or instructions set by adults (e.g. 'No Ball Games'). The environment should be open enough and with resources enough to support freedom of symbolic expression, be that vocal, physical, dramatic, creative and destructive, through the provision and availability of relevant materials and spaces. Other features could be a rock to stand on, a dark cave to shout or perform in, or a row of windows in a derelict factory that invites playful destruction. Armitage (2001) has shown that school playgrounds that appear boring to adult eyes hold a plethora of special spaces for children, including the tiggy spot, the prison, the witches' cauldron, the solitary/quiet spot and, on wet days, the puddle.

Varied natural environments are the best for play, as such environments support the play of components within that environment, be they elemental (air, earth, fire, water; light/dark, hot/cold) or the interplay of a variety of elements or 'loose parts' (Nicholson 1971). In one sense all environments are 'natural' in that humans use them and play within them; however, small plots of land with a variety of plants, trees and grasses are often more preferable to acres of tarmac or concrete slabs. Nicholson's theory (1971) works on the idea that the more variables there are in an environment, the more opportunities for interaction and play within it; put simply, few bits = less play, lots of bits = more play.

Natural environments are also good for children to find special places, what the old ones used to call *temenos*, sacred places and *liminal* spaces, thresholds to other worlds. Every environment offers spaces and experiences for the player to gain pleasure, however children may have to look harder or be more imaginative in 'concrete jungles'. These special places are often symbolic, metaphorical or sometimes intangible, offering an 'otherworldliness', an 'as if' ability that encourages the player to 'suspend disbelief' and engage with mysterious and new experiences. Fairy rings in the grass do this naturally, as do bridges across streams. Often children may be drawn to quiet or remote parts of their neighbourhoods to access these special places, which may be self-made dens where normal rules do not apply, chalk circles or simply stones in the ground that children invest with a special, sacred power. These spaces act as gateways into the children's play world, helping them create magic all around them.

Overall the environment is where play takes place, and it is important for play that the individual feels the environment is theirs for the duration of their play, and all external evaluation is absent – the play is the child's; we should walk with baby steps all around it lest our big boots crush the tender shoots of play.

A setting's approach to play and children

> Children learn what they need to survive in the culture they are born to, and what they learn – or fail to learn – faithfully echoes wider cultural values.
>
> *Jay Griffiths (2013: 173)*

Griffiths reminds us that what adults value is reflected in the provision we make (or don't make) for children; if we value self-expression, children will experience and learn about self-expression; if we value 'free play' then children will find provision that welcomes them and allows them to freely express themselves. If we value control and safety, then the provision will be designed to permit certain types of behaviour towards those planned outcomes.

In reality, most settings, whether staffed or not, will be a balance of values and expected outcomes, based on government expectations, the philosophy of the setting and the demands of customers. The experience of the setting for children and adults will be an interplay of these various elements, with different ones taking precedence at times. Some of these criteria are shown in Table 4.2.

When planning provision of play, if we work towards ensuring that activities are self-chosen, engaging and satisfying, then the setting may have more elements of the left side of Table 4.2. If the setting is a care setting designed to meet the needs of adults, or with an educational focus, it may have more elements of the right side of the table. Asking how any space for play meets these criteria will help providers decide on the value and purpose of the setting.

Table 4.2 Criteria for determining a setting's approach to play and children.

Chosen by child	....	Decided by adult
Free choice of activity	....	Adult-directed programme
Improves child's life	....	Improves adult's life
Play centred	....	Limited play
Learning emergent	....	Skills focused
Free to come and go	....	Care service
No cost	....	Pay per session
No adults	....	Adults always present

It may be seen that wild places, woods, fields and beaches tend to meet more of the criteria of the left side of the table, and while these elements may be more conducive to self-chosen play, many adults and some children would feel that the places were 'unsafe' or too risky without adult supervision and risk management. If the aim is to provide, say, out-of-school care, residential holidays or hospital play, then more of the right-side elements may be present, but if the elements *Play centred* and *Free choice of activity* are still present, then the setting may be considered to support play. Some of these criteria are relatively objective, others will require a judgement to be made by those present; the point of the criteria is to guide those in control of a space to understand why they are making choices the way that they do.

As explained above, in many parts of the world no provision is made for children to play, and yet they still do and appear to be basically functional human beings. It might seem that a return to 'natural play' in the west may be what is required or desired. Yet, after generations of industrialization, horticultural development, enclosure, urban development, social changes and media comment, it seems naive to simply let children go 'back to nature'; what is *natural* about the environment that most children in westernized societies are exposed to? Some might argue that as humans are experts at adapting an environment to meet their needs, then the surroundings that we have created in urban spaces are 'natural' to us. Others argue that while the argument is valid, we need to take a longer view; the most recent large-scale evolutionary change was around 20,000 years ago when humans moved from a hunter–gatherer form of existence to an agricultural one. Our bodies, skills and abilities have been shaped by the need to walk upright, chase and tend animals, use tools, communicate with others, and assess and solve complex problems over time. Those skills and abilities still dominate but have been tempered by our developing cognitive abilities and technological adaptations. While a return to medieval forms of labour and agriculture would not be seen as desirable for many people, neither should a life spent in front of a computer or video screen be seen as appropriate for human beings; a question of balance is needed to help adults and children use their minds and bodies.

With the benefit of post-modern thinking we can see that environments are not just physical spaces but are shaped through a complex interaction of resources, relationships, policies, practices, habits, procedures, symbols, feelings and beliefs that act together to influence spaces of all kinds; these different forces can be explained by using the Integral Play Framework.

Application of the Integral Play Framework to spaces for play

In brief, when supporting children's playing, provision and space for play should be based on the needs of the child, as facilitated by adults, through the provision and within the laws and policies of the city/country in which those spaces are found.

The Integral Play Framework helps adults providing for play to realize that children need spaces that meet their play needs, physical as well as relational, cognitive and creative as well as cultural. Adults will be in control of the opportunities to make good or neglect the physical infrastructure, they will influence relationships by the values they share or oppose, they will uphold or attack rights according to local conditions and global laws, and they will constrain opportunities for expression and enchantment, or they will delight and fascinate with magical spaces and invitations. Adults who support children's play should give them spaces to run around, resources to express themselves, a chance to be in a group and alone, the opportunity to work things through at their own pace and in their own way – see Figure 4.1.

In what may be seen as an extension of Bronfenbrenner's model (1979), the Integral Play Framework can be used to look at the different forms of support that adults can offer to playing children. Wherever they are, children are able to play in the spaces available. These spaces will be influenced by local conditions such as the adults and others in or adjacent to those spaces. The quality of the play experience will be affected by how the child uses the space, their influence on it, and the influences of others on the space and the behaviour of

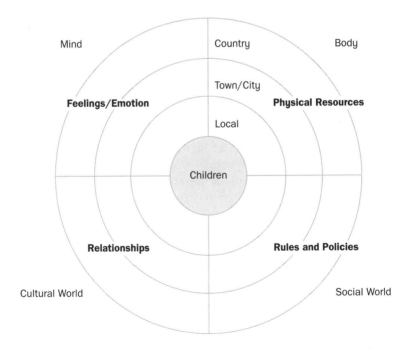

Figure 4.1 Integral Play Framework and spaces for play.

the child. Examples of others in the space could be parents and siblings at home, teachers and other pupils in school, or neighbours and friends in the street. Each of these examples will be affected by how the child is able to move around, express their opinions, how confident they feel with others and how they feel about the rules imposed on that part of their world. They will also be affected by how others, usually adults, make physical space available or supporting of play, the rules they set on the space, the relationships expected in the space, and the range of emotions and expressions allowed there. These influences will be present where the child is, in the local environments, within the town or city the space is in, and will be affected by the laws and policies of the relevant country.

Typically, children in countries like the UK will have more influence and freedom at home, often with limited room; they will have less influence and freedom at school, though usually more space at playtime, and they will have varied amounts of influence and freedom in the street and local neighbour-hood, and usually much more varied space (though not always) if able to roam in the wider community. The norms of the town and country will also encroach upon what is 'normal' for that space. While all of a country's laws, ethics and freedoms are expected to apply throughout the country, in reality each home, neighbourhood and district has a localized version of those expec-tations. The worst and probably most extreme example would be the child in an abusive home, where the individual child's legal rights may be severely curtailed by an adult's behaviour if not identified and challenged by neigh-bours or local officials. More typically, while there may be countrywide expectations and standards, local variations in schools or towns will be affected by the localized culture created by the leaders and staff in those areas and by the availability of local resources and finances. For example, it may be recognized that playing outdoors and in nature is valuable for chil-dren, yet settings can limit this, justifying it by lack of resources or limited space, or occasionally lack of effort by those in control of the setting. The model shows us that in supporting provision for children's playing, all these influences would ideally be working towards the needs and desires of the playing child; however, the reality is very different for most children.

Supporting children's play

The Integral Play Framework helps with understand the different opportuni-ties that should be available in settings whether staffed or not (Table 4.3). A tool for evaluating these opportunities is explained later, in Chapter 8.

Provision for children's emotionally based play should help with percep-tion and sensation (the private, internal world of the child); it should recog-nize the importance of intuition by children and in work with children. There are stories that help children understand the world; these stories may be universal in theme yet different in each culture – how can we support children through story and symbol making, especially traditional stories? Creativity is important in children's lives, both for the fun and satisfaction it brings to the child, but also as a prerequisite for problem solving; without creativity we are in danger of simply restating others' solutions. Children unusually rationalize the world from their own perspective; by offering new experiences and new viewpoints we can help children appreciate others' views and ways of seeing the world.

Looking at interactions with others, provision is often based on the beliefs and values of the adults operating it; can those present in an environment learn to respect others' beliefs in a non-judgmental, open way rather than simply because of a desire to comply with equal opportunities legislation? Can we understand that children will necessarily go through a stage of independence and rebelling, as well as mirroring, copying and conforming to the expectations of others, prior to sharing ideas and feelings with others – through imagination, drama, music and stories. Inevitably, children will test these ideas against others, rebelling against the norms in order to

Table 4.3 Supporting children's play – offering different opportunities.

	The 'internal' world	The 'external' world
Me (My world)	• Rationalizing • Problem solving – creativity • Expressing satisfaction • Feeling enjoyment • Stories – symbols; fantasy • Intuiting • Perceiving – sensation	• Prototyping – mastery • Designing • Coordinating movements and actions – balance (subtle); delicate actions • Adapting • Running, jumping, balancing (gross); strength, movement, speed • Exploring – smell, touch, taste, sight, sound
Us (Our world)	• Solitary activity • Following others • Copying – role-play • Sharing and joint creation – imagination, drama, music, stories • Mirroring – copying and conforming • Independent – rebelling • Respecting beliefs	• Working alone • Friends – communication • Groups – families, protecting • Team activities – cooperating with others • Roles – competition • Leading – leadership; caring

become independent and autonomous, confident in what they believe and respectful of others' beliefs. These actions may be challenging for adults, though the more open and authentic we can be, the better for the child and ultimately society. As with all these opportunities, the adult is not needed to make them happen, but an insensitive or authoritarian approach to the child may constrain or prevent such activities from taking place. While children can play just around the corner from their homes in streets or 'slack spaces', increasingly disapproving neighbours can force them to move on or change their behaviour.

Play spaces are most commonly based on what can be seen as simple physical experiences: exploring – smell, touch, taste, sight, sound, and running, jumping, simple balancing, strength, movement, speed. Some environments give children the opportunity to change and adapt spaces – for example, through sand boxes and den building; some the chance to design or destroy the things they play with, most usually in settings like adventure playgrounds, but also in settings using forest school approaches. As children grow up, they welcome the chance to coordinate their movements and actions through subtle balance and delicate actions, throwing and catching, using tools and instruments. This may be facilitated by a climbable tree or purpose-built climbing frame. Having control over their environment may lead to experimenting, prototyping new ways of interacting and joining with the world and so, perhaps, mastery over what is there.

In the shared social space with others, children need the chance to play alone and with friends communicating both through voice and body. As younger children they will form family bonds with those close to them; later on they may extend these relationships with others in their communities at home, at school and in the neighbourhood. Through these relationships they will experience care and protection, competition and leadership, changing roles in different places, being in charge, making decisions or following others at other times.

These lists are not meant to be read as curricula or programmes for settings. They are intended to demonstrate the complexity of human play and how pigeonholing play as simply physical or social can limit the experiences a child needs as they go through the world.

> Play is the means by which young mammals practice the skills they must develop in order to survive and reproduce. These include physical skills, such as chasing down prey or avoiding predators; social skills required to get along with others of their kind; and emotional skills, such as those required to control fear and anger in tense situations. Children even more than other young mammals, learn physical, social and emotional skills through play.
>
> *Peter Gray (2013: 278)*

And we might add the cultural beliefs and values of the communities in which they live, for they will have an impact on children's play and lives as well. Children will learn to comply with or challenge cultural norms depending on the values of the adults in those cultures. Some religions will welcome challenging questions and viewpoints, others will expect compliance; some communities will expect children to be 'seen and not heard', others will value free expression.

Gray (2013: 279) also comments, in an update on play in modern societies, that children in industrial cultures will play with mechanical functions and roles, and children in the twenty-first century will play with technology and computers. By implication children in less industrialized nations will play with and learn about care of animals, planting seeds, harvesting and the seasons of the year. Environments, whether designed for play, 'natural' or urban, will offer wide-ranging opportunities for interaction and play, some of which children will be able to take advantage of, others that will be out of their reach physically or for other reasons.

Varied opportunities for play of all kinds

To help with children talking their play as far as they wish, provision for play should also contain a variety of what James Gibson called *affordances* (1977), to offer as many play opportunities as possible. All environments have affordances or capacity for interaction, yet accessing them will vary from child to child and as the child grows. A flat tarmac playground affords chances for running about and space for children to gather but not to go higher, under or through; a grassed area with bushes gives the chance for more interactions with nature and things to hide behind or among but it's not so good for a game of football. Gibson defined affordances as 'possibilities for action' present in the environment, though dependent on the capabilities of the person using them. A space may have a frame or wall that children could climb on, provided that the gap between levels is appropriate to their abilities; a high gap would not afford climbing for a toddler or for someone with limited mobility. Sand or water areas may not offer chances for exploration if they are out of reach or poorly maintained.

Varied affordances in the environment make it possible for children to interact, use and play with that space according to their own needs. Varied levels, heights, materials, resources and experiences allow children to choose how far they want to take their play. If the experiences are limited then children may never go as far as they are capable, or may get frustrated with the opportunities on offer in a space. The Integral Play Framework suggests that, as children explore their environment, begin to move through it and gain mastery in what they can do, they will need new experiences for them to discover and experience. To fully meet children's growing needs, environments that support play should offer a variety of affordances for exploring mental and cognitive play, physical play, artistic and cultural play, role-playing and social play. Experiences should be diverse and graduated to help children move from one event to another. A frame with fixed steps becomes relatively easy to climb once the first step has been covered; a structure with varied dimensions between levels takes a little bit more thought and competence to climb well. Some settings offer children 'painting by numbers' images to colour, yet a blank piece of paper with a variety of colouring sources and pencils will offer more possibilities for children to be artistic and creative, provided it is available in an environment free of uncritical judgements.

Helping ensure all play needs are met

When planning for children's play environments, there has often been an unconscious focus on the children's physical and social play, because those are the types of play that can most readily be observed. Using the Integral Play Framework, we can see what might be missing in any given plan of play spaces.

Hughes created his 'criteria for a rich play environment' (1996b) to give an indication of the kinds of elements that play provision should offer. Casey extended this list with the features of enriching, inclusive spaces (2007). These two lists have been merged and allocated a place in the Integral Play Framework according to the overall emphasis of the measure (see Table 4.4).

Table 4.4 Elements for play provision mapped on to the Integral Play Framework

Mind	Body
	Accessibility – physical
	Centres of interest
	Continuity between indoors and outdoors
	Elements – earth, air, fire, water
	Manipulating fabricated and natural materials
	Movement
Atmosphere	Natural features
Experiencing a range of emotions	Stimulation of the five senses
	Shelter
	Sufficient space

Cultural world	Social world
Accessibility – cultural	Accessibility – economic/social
Playing with identity	Social interactions

Overall criteria
Flexible and creative
Interesting and varied
Risk and challenge

Most of the criteria have been located, though three criteria were overarching and could be said to apply to any quadrant; these were *Flexible and creative, Interesting and varied,* and *Risk and challenge.*

The table shows an imbalance between the various sides of the model in that most criteria are related to the observable, objective world of bodies and society, how bodies are used and how they work and how humans relate to one another; the subjective emotional and cultural elements are hardly covered. Using the Framework it becomes relatively easy to add in the missing elements such as opportunities for drama, music and storytelling, local cultural elements and an understanding that children will want/need to express their emotions in a variety of ways, from very quiet to very loud.

The Framework also helps us understand the different challenges for children with differing needs. In Casey's list (2007) she identified accessibility as a necessary element, however, when looking at access we can use the medical (physical) model or the social (cultural) model. The medical/physical model looks at the biomechanics involved – those that do not function within 'normal parameters' need some form of separate provision to meet their needs. The social model rejects the medical approach, and recognizes that it is society that disables those with impairments due to the way they are treated through comparisons with others and expectations of behaviour and ability. The Framework helps us identify that, while access may be physical and can be accommodated by the provision of slopes, more handrails or varied colours, and so on, social barriers may be cultural (i.e. the way we value others), but also economic (i.e. it may cost more to accommodate those with additional needs) and societal (the roles we expect people to take in society). In play children will often accept and then overcome any barriers in their way – it is part of growing up – provided that any adults also in the play space understand what is happening and try not to 'rescue' them.

Supporting settings in different ways

The more 'play literate' we are as adults who support children playing, the more our reflections and interventions may be based on our own thoughts and feelings, but also on current practice and theory. The more we know, the better skills we have, the more we can intervene appropriately with actions based on our knowledge of the benefits of play for the child and the myriad ways that play might manifest. We might never know what the child's motivation for playing was, but by being aware of the possibilities with play and how that play might be valuable for a given child, we might get closer to a 'proper' play-supporting response.

By recognizing that play is a process, we also need to recognize that our response should be a process as well. If we over-analyse what has happened, we are looking backwards in time to something that happened 'then' and not what is happening 'now'. We need to work 'in the moment', based on our thoughts, feelings and experiences; we also need to expand those thoughts, feelings and experiences as best we can, within the resources and time at our disposal.

Supporting provision for playing children – managers and funders

Often when making provision for children's play, much emphasis is put on how the adults and staff should relate to children. It follows that in addition to face-to-face workers, people supporting, managing or funding play settings while not directly interacting with children should recognize the value of play in children's lives. To this end, managers and funders should:

- recognize the child's right to play (Article 31 of the United Nations Convention on the Rights of the Child)
- support and facilitate the play process through their work, recognizing that the impulse to play is innate within children
- respect the right of children to decide and control the content and intent of their play
- recognize that the play process is vital for the child and will take precedence over adult agendas.

While espousing support for Article 31, too frequently managers and funders do not understand or value good play practice. Children need to play and will choose experiences that meet their play needs, yet too often the opportunity for self-chosen, engaging activity is denied children as 'adults know best'. For children play is important and they prioritize it in their lives over other more adult considerations such as being responsible, following instructions, working to the rules. For managers and funders play is often seen as part of education, and that child safety (and education and well-being) is paramount. Adults also felt they could influence play for the better or to produce better outcomes, so adult intervention was necessary to ensure safety or 'help' the children do well. Of course this would adulterate or contaminate the play, albeit with well-meaning intentions.

The national play agency Play Wales (2013) clarified the role of adults in supporting children's play; many of the criteria it listed, while not just applying to managers or funders, reflected good practice with children as it saw it, as follows.

- We must listen to what children say about their play and genuinely value their contributions.
- We must consider children's play spaces as important environments that should be protected.

- We should advocate that children's play is essential for healthy development and well-being. It is a legitimate behaviour and their human right and this applies to children playing indoors and outdoors.

- Children's play is often chaotic, frantic and noisy, and children's play spaces are often messy, disordered and idiosyncratic. We need to understand that children's conception of a desirable play space does not look like an adult's. We need to be tolerant of mess and dirt!

- We can support children's play by providing loose parts and rejecting over-commercialism.

- We can prioritize children's time to play freely. If we over-supervise or over-protect we take away the child's free choice and the very thing that makes their behaviour play.

Play Wales (2013)

Supporting provision for playing children – local and central government

One of the biggest problems for playing children outside of provision or settings that support play is many other people in the environment have opinions about children playing out, and they are mostly negative. Many adults subscribe to the Victorian view that 'children should be seen and not heard'.

In the UK, schools have had to curtail playtime or erect soundproof barriers to prevent upsetting neighbours, young children have been cautioned by police officers for chalking on pavements, and children as young as 3 or 4 have received warning letters from police for 'intimidating' and 'anti-social' behaviour because they played outside (Metro 2013). While there are local initiatives to try to challenge these attitudes, there has been little in recent years from governments to challenge prevailing views.

Despite the billions of pounds poured annually into relevant services for children in the UK and elsewhere, politicians might consider that current priorities for children are not as effective as they might wish. Surveys across Europe and the USA show increasing unhappiness (UNICEF 2007, 2013), the lowering of both well-being and comparative educational achievement in the UK's children (Child Poverty Action Group 2009) compared to countries like Finland, which have a much more playful approach to education (Sahlberg 2012). The growing evidence of the benefits of play for children (Lester and Russell 2010) should help inform policy decisions, yet it seems like a severe provocation in many UK and USA government departments. If children were seen less as mini-adults in need of an education for employment, and needing excessive protection from the dangers of the world, they might enjoy life a little more, become more adaptable and resilient, and more flexible and skilled in making a contribution to the problems humanity has brought upon the world in the twenty-first century. A little more real choice for children, a little more respect for them as citizens in their own right and a bit more respect for the role of play in their lives might go a long way.

Good practice for local and central government officers and politicians would include:

- recognizing the child's right to play (Article 31 of the United Nations Convention on the Rights of the Child)
- recognizing that the play process is vital for the child in their childhood and also for later benefits in life
- respecting the right of children to decide and control the content and intent of their play.

Good news arrived in 2013 with the *United Nations Convention on the Rights of the Child – General Comment No. 17 (2013) on Article 31* (Lansdown 2013). Article 31 covers the right of the child to rest, leisure, play, recreational activities, cultural life and the arts. The purpose of the General Comment was to set out what governments are required to do to implement the different parts of the convention they have signed.

The General Comment defined all elements of Article 31, in addition to the statement on play, and explained their importance to the growth and development of children and their impact on children's overall well-being. In the 22-page General Comment statement, challenges to the implementation of Article 31 were addressed. These included lack of awareness of adults of its importance (particularly of child-controlled play), inadequate space, excessive pressure for educational achievement, increase in structured and programmed leisure time, as well as negative effects of technology, and the fact that children are rarely involved in planning for play (this referred to UNCRC Article 12 – respect for the views of the child). Attention was also given to groups of children requiring particular attention in order to realize their rights under Article 31. Children with disabilities, girl children, children in institutions, working children and children in extreme poverty were examples of these. The General Comment provided a detailed elaboration of the specific actions that governments needed to take to ensure that all the provisions of Article 31 were fully implemented. The General Comment calls on 'states parties' to support the statement – i.e. the governing bodies of all the world's countries (except the USA, South Sudan and Somalia, which have yet to sign up to the Convention).

Of course the merit of the statement will be proven when states' parties embrace the challenges in the document and make the right to play a reality in their country.

One country that is setting a good example in this regard is Wales, where the aim is to make Wales a 'play-friendly place'. In support of this and in addition to the *Welsh Assembly Government Play Policy* (2002), Wales has brought into legislation *The Play Sufficiency Assessment Regulations 2012*.

The Play Sufficiency Assessment requires all local authorities in the country to demonstrate consideration of the range of factors that affect children's opportunities to play. These included demographic profiles of the area, assessments of open space and existing and potential play space, dedicated play provision, and recreational provision, and other factors that promoted play opportunities including planning, traffic, transport, information and publicity, and workforce development (Welsh Government/Play Wales 2012). At the time of writing, this initiative was still in its beginning stages, but was certainly a healthy development in the move to help those responsible for the public realm to recognize the complexity of children's play and how small changes can have dramatic effects on the lives of children.

Another example is the *Child in the City Movement*, which started in 2002 and aims to make cities more 'child friendly': 'If we are concerned about the future of any city, we must consider how to involve children in its network, and in its economic and social life. And the best way to involve children is through play – children are really experts at playing' (Child in the City 2012). Sadly, this movement has a long way to go, for as Colin Ward said more than 30 years ago, 'I don't want a Childhood City. I want a city where children live in the same world I do . . . We have enormous expertise and a mountain of research on the appropriate provision of parks and play-spaces for use by children of different ages, but the ultimate truth is that children play anywhere and everywhere' (Ward 1978). If we can improve cities for children, we end up improving them for everyone, but it would mean deprioritizing the car so that people can move around without fear of being killed.

The answer is as shown by the Netherlands (and some other parts of Europe), where priority is given to pedestrians and cyclists in inner-city areas. Motorized vehicle drivers can drive at high speeds on autobahns and designated urban clearways, yet must give way to cyclists and pedestrians when in built-up areas and near homes. If a road accident occurs in the home environment, the car driver is considered responsible; not unreasonable if we consider that a car can harm a cyclist or pedestrian much more than they can hurt the car. Again such a change would require a lead from government, as took place with the wearing of seat-belts in vehicles and stopping smoking in public places in the UK and some other countries. The change of legislation could be effected in a year and would soon become usual practice, but many countries including the UK and USA place too high a value on cars at the current time.

Supporting children's play is a complex business as they can play in any environment, at any time but, as we have seen, when the child's play needs are considered at every level it is possible to make spaces more play friendly and so more child friendly; adults have a big part to play in this as we will explore in the subsequent chapters.

Questions to help practitioners when supporting spaces and provision for play

- Can you list five significant and varied reasons why provision should be made for children's play? Using the Integral Play Framework can you list the key elements that should be provided in a park playground, a primary school and a town/city centre play space?
- Looking at three play spaces that you are familiar with, can you assess whose needs are being meet though the service – children's or adults? Can you share your findings with your staff team or your neighbours and discuss the implications of that? What will you do with the outcomes of your discussion?
- What elements would be needed in order to be able to support a balanced offer for playing children in your setting or community? Which activities would cause you/your colleagues the greatest anxiety? What could you do about that? Parents believe it is in their children's best interests to keep them safe in the house or garden; do you agree?

5

Interacting with playing children

To talk about 'interactive play' is as redundant as to talk about 'interactive conversation'. Of course a conversation is interactive, since it involves at least two people making choices, engaging with meanings external to themselves, and responding to them. Play is not different from this: it is an invitation to you to engage with a different world, a world of your and someone else's imagination. Without your active engagement in that invitation, nothing happens.

After Brian Eno (1996: 401)

Building on an extensive definition of play and a description of the Integral Play Framework, we have looked at how others value play and how to provide spaces that support play and playing. This chapter will consider how to interact with playing children using models and descriptions common in the UK. The approach is based 'in the moment', and aims to help adults and workers with playing children assess what is happening *now* in their and to a lesser extent the child's 'being' – it is an approach that values process over rules. The roles that adults can take in interacting and supporting children will be explored, with a few examples from practice.

How children play: a snapshot using the ten essentials of playing

In Chapter 1, the *Essential Characteristics of Playing* were explained, based on an analysis of several play theorists. But what might an adult see when children are playing; how might the adult interpret what is happening for the child?

First, we need to remember that play is a process, not a specific action. Play occurs when a child (or other human) wants to play; it requires a space in which to play but does not require another player, or an adult to supervise or guide the play. Play may be energetic or passive, loud or quiet; it may be social or solitary, emotional or coolly calculating. How can adults hoping to support or understand play make sense of that? The Integral Play Framework goes some way to explaining why children may explore different domains in their play. Different types of play affect children in different ways; some forms of play require a lot of physical energy, others a lot of emotional or mental energy. Children's play encompasses the vital domains of humanity – physical, emotional, cognitive, belief based and relational.

Children in their play will not consciously play for what adults see as the benefits of play; benefits may arise from the variety and frequency of play types that children enjoy but cannot be predicted. The play is theirs; they will play for reasons we can guess at but never really know. Play will be affected by the children's thoughts, moods, abilities and their interactions – both physical and emotional – with the world around them. When confident, their 'play cues' (Sturrock and Else 1998) will be many and extended; when less confident, the cues may be subtle or infrequent. Understanding children's play helps adults describe and reflect on children's actions and interactions.

For actions to be playful they need to be unforced, self-chosen engagement, and with a willingness to participate. The player has expectations of the action (something might happen), they may be a 'willing beginner', open to experiences, and prepared to act in response to what emerges. This action is spontaneous, of the moment, freely chosen, yet with personal constraints of ability, confidence and experience, whether known or unknown to the player.

The player will be actively engaged in their play, paying attention to the immediate feedback gained, responding and adapting as necessary for the play to continue if desired, or end if the actions are unrewarding or if circumstances change.

For this to take place the player should feel relatively stress-free at the moment of play – all other threats are forgotten in the moment of play. The player will be 'sufficiently' safe physically and psychologically (Else, after Rogers 1961), for some activities may take the player into danger, yet if they feel in control they will still engage with the activity. Learning to ride a bike is not without harm but when children are willing to try it, they endure the accompanying bruises and scrapes; doing a drawing might be playful if self-chosen, copying a picture because someone told you to might not be.

When playing, the player is usually engaging with a whole body/mind experience in the play. Thoughts will be guiding actions, sensations will be forming feelings, and feeling will result in pleasure and attachments (or otherwise). The playing child does not do this consciously; the activity is a seamless blend of actions, feelings, thoughts and relationships.

Because of this 'lack of consciousness' play is often timeless; the player is immersed in the play, 'lost in the moment', not conscious of the passing of time – 'time flies when you are having fun'.

Part of the big appeal of playing is curiosity; being attracted to newness or new experiences. The player is actively engaged in their play, which may result in surprise 'A-ha!' moments, reverie or new actions, new feelings, new experiences. For some children, experiencing snow for the first time can be a magical experience, for others playing with new people, or in new situations, and for some overcoming a challenge or completing a long awaited activity is the attraction.

When these characteristics come together the result is that the player gains pleasurable sensations from the playing, which may range from the subtle to the gross, may last for microseconds or several hours, be quiet satisfaction with a themed activity or a brief belly laugh.

As has been discussed, the player plays for their own reasons, which are many and varied and may be conscious, subconscious or unconscious, known, unknown or unknowable. The drive to play and therefore the manifestation of the play will be different for each person – the moment, the duration, the aspects involved. For this reason the experience and therefore the benefit of playing will be different for each child, even when playing the same game. The player is not driven by extrinsic goals, though they may agree to play along with them; satisfaction is self-defined.

While it helps to consider each of these ten essential characteristics of playing – or more simply choice, engagement and satisfaction – the adult can support and influence the child's experience of playing, by making environmental changes and by choosing when to intervene or respond to the playing child; understanding the play cycle will help with responding appropriately.

Understanding the play cycle

The *play cycle* (sometimes called the *play process* – Sturrock and Else 1998) helps explain both the repetitive and developing nature of play. The play cycle also shows that playing can be disrupted or altered if the process is interrupted.

The play cycle was first conceptualized by Gordon Sturrock for his MA thesis, and was later adapted and published (Sturrock and Else 1998) in the academic paper, 'The playground as therapeutic space: playwork as healing' presented at the IPA/USA Triennial National Conference held at Longmont, Colorado, USA. The fundamental premise in the paper was that if incidents in childhood have the potential to create trauma, then playing through those incidents as they happen or soon afterwards has therapeutic effect. The Integral Play Framework extended the original idea into the physical, social and cultural domains; if children do not play as they need to they will potentially become 'stuck', rather than adaptive and flexible across a variety of skills and situations.

Since then, the *Colorado Paper* (as it became known) has been the basis of many key papers in the playwork field and adopted into working language in the UK and wider afield. Integrating and adapting ideas from other thinkers (notably Gregory Bateson, Erving Goffman, C.G. Jung and D.W. Winnicott), the paper outlined *psycholudics* – the study of the mind and psyche at play – aiming to describe 'the process of play as it happens'. This approach has been used and delivered on many courses and presentations in the UK, Sweden, Australia and other countries, and was used in part as underpinning knowledge for the UK's Playwork Principles, 'the professional and ethical framework for playwork' (PPSG 2005). A full explanation of the play cycle would take a book by itself, yet the basic concepts may be explained succinctly and will help adults working with playing children better understand the process taking place.

In brief the play cycle is started when the child wants to play and issues a play cue; a play frame is formed and a play return is experienced. That may result in play flow, whereby the cycle of cues and return is established, or the play may be annihilated if the child finds the return unsatisfactory or threatening (Sturrock and Else 1998). This process is shown in Figure 5.1. In the diagram, the child is represented by the darker circle on the left, everything that is not the child (others and the environment) by the lighter circle on the right. The interlinked smaller circles represent the play drive, the conscious and yet unconscious desire to play. The arrows indicate varied play cues of differing strengths and duration, both from the child and the other player in the environment. The dotted line suggests the play frame; annihilation is not shown as the diagram shows play flow between two players.

If adults working with playing children understand that the play cue is initiated by the child, then half the battle is won; the child will be choosing what to play with. When the child experiences a 'good enough' play cue they

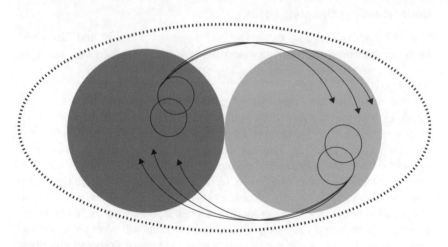

Figure 5.1 The play cycle.

Source: Sturrock and Else (1998).

will be engaged and involved in the play and will continue it until they are satisfied by the activity. Of course the child could get an unsatisfactory play return and the play would immediately end or change into something else; not every play cue is successful, nor is every play return appropriate.

Without knowing more of this model, it should help adults support children's play, especially if the responses that the adult offers are evaluated and reflected on, ideally with others in the play space. However, a detailed understanding of the process may help with discussion to help improve our response to children playing. The process starts with the play drive.

Play drive or impulse The child's *play drive* or play instinct functions through an interplay with the surrounding environment or ecology. The impulse to play will be affected by the child's sense of identity and power (or lack of power), values, beliefs, level of thought and understanding, physical skill and ability.

This drive to play is intrinsic to the child and is manifested in the play cue.

Play cue The *play cue* is the signal the child gives that they want to play.

This cue may be spoken, eye contact, a body signal or by the use of materials. The play cue comes from the thoughts of the child, their internal world, into the physical world in the expectation of getting a response.

A child kicking a ball towards you is a play cue; you are expected to kick it back. Picking up a paintbrush, singing a song and starting a conversation could all be play cues. Children invite participation by other children or adults in their play by communicating feelings, thoughts and intentions. And children may also simply play with the environment, if the play cue (action) creates a change in the environment that the child finds curious or interesting, they may be inclined to repeat or extend that action to 'see what happens'. Children can choose to play the same game over and over again as long as they are getting what they need from that action. They can also adapt, extend or stop the cycle by changing the play or by responding (cuing) in different ways. The play cue takes place within the play frame.

Play frame The *play frame* is the boundary, physical or thematic, that keeps the play intact.

The play frame is initiated and 'chosen' by the child, and is the 'enclosure' for their playful expression. A child building a sand castle uses the sand tray or square metre of sand on a beach for that activity; the action is constrained by the scale of what they want to do. The size and scope of the play frame will be determined by the confidence the child has in the environment they play in; the more the child feels able to exert choice without coming to harm, the more likely they are to extend the play frame.

For example, a child on a beach could range quite a distance from their friends or family in their desire to build more or larger sandcastles, and sand often finds its way out of a sand tray, though this is not always welcomed by staff in settings.

The play frame will be supported or contained by the physical boundaries of the available play space (as explained above), or it may be constrained by the themes of the child's play. The theme of the play may not contain the play physically, but it may constrain the actions or choices in the play – for example, it is not usual for children role-playing a home scenario to suddenly blast off into space (not usual but not impossible!). The frame is not dependent upon and may or may not synchronize with physical or thematic boundaries.

The child may change the frame by including others, moving objects or adapting it in some other way to create a varied response (return) that maintains the play flow.

Play flow *Play flow* occurs when the frame has been established and the child becomes 'lost' in their play. Children at play are 'alive in the moment', with no concern for the past or future. Once entered into, this play flow can absorb the child or children over minutes or days at a time.

The play may cover a number of topics in a few moments, with roles changing, ideas developing and concepts shifting, or it could be the single focus on a particular aspect. The play becomes self-regulated and any adults, if not actually playing with the child, are largely outside of the play frame. Play flow is reliant on the playing child satisfactorily gaining feedback from play returns.

Play return (play response) The *play return* is the response the child experiences as a result of the play cue. The play return will be experienced by the playing child from the environment or as initiated by another child or adult. It is what the child experiences after they issue the play cue.

The child will choose what to 'play' with. The return will usually come back from another child or adult; they will be playing together, though the child can also find a return from the environment around them. They may be digging for treasure in the sandpit; they may be hunting for insects in the bushes. If the child gets a positive response they may choose to extend and enhance that experience by issuing another cue; they will be playing, gaining feedback and experiencing satisfaction. If the child gets a negative response they may stop playing or try another play cue. Understanding this process helps adults offer choices to the child to help them maintain or extend the play.

When the return is initiated by an adult, it should be made with an awareness of the child's emotional state, cultural understanding, physical abilities and sense of power (as far as they can be known) and primarily the adult's own cultural understanding and sense of power. The aim should be to support the child's play, not replace it with actions of the adult. If the adult gets it wrong, the child will quickly annihilate the play cue and so end the play cycle.

Annihilation *Play annihilation* is the end of the play for the child at that time. This may be a simple end to the game (everyone has been caught) or a dramatic destruction of the model or sandcastle they have spent the last hour carefully constructing.

Annihilation will occur when the play has no more meaning for the child, when the child has got whatever they were looking for from the play experience. Adults working with children can often misunderstand this. Workers can be dismayed when a piece of art, instead of being mounted and displayed on the wall, is painted over and thrown in the bin; for the child it may be more about the doing than the producing. Annihilation is about the child taking their choice in the play to a natural conclusion.

Understanding psycholudics

To take our interacting with playing children a stage further, it can be useful to understand psycholudics in more depth. A complete glossary of psycholudic terms is included in Appendix 3.

> The *ludido*, the play drive, could be precisely seen as the active agency of an evolving consciousness – such a description is closer to the definitions out of eastern psychologies and traditions, the *lila* principle – in what we call a 'field' or psychic, ludic ecology.
>
> *Gordon Sturrock (1996)*

As with the libido (the sex drive), the *ludido* (the drive to play) is determined by biological, psychological and social factors: what can the player do, how do they feel about it, and what is permitted in the surrounding culture and society.

The ludido functions through an interplay with the surrounding elements, which circulate through the *metalude*, the 'unconsciously conscious' thought that precedes any playful act, the moment of daydreaming or reverie that sets out the intent of the play; it is formed in the mind of the child and shapes the play cues that go to the external, physical world. It is described as *unconsciously conscious* as the child might be interested in a particular activity and feel that a choice has been made as to what to play with, yet that choice will depend on many factors such as feeling sufficiently safe, curiosity, anticipated pleasure, and ability and skill to do what is required; not all of these 'considerations' will be processed consciously. The term metalude also suggests the 'playfulness of play' in that it crosses boundaries and motifs in microseconds; it can, and does, go anywhere and everywhere according to whim and feedback – a chase game becomes a play-fight, becomes a chat, becomes a story becomes a chase game again, and so on.

The *ludic ecology* is the space for play (both physical, bounded by the environment and psychic, bounded by the themes, thoughts and feelings of the player). It is not a solid formation, but a mobile, flexible extension, where options, ideas and themes change and adapt in contact with the surrounding, supporting and containing environment. 'Options, ideas, themes', which will be instinctive, conscious and unconscious, using actions, feelings, thoughts and metaphors as necessary and as appropriate. The 'field of play' is freely accessed by the child according to desires and drives both impulsive and chosen; it will be relatively stress free – if the child feels threatened physically or psychologically, play is unlikely to occur. The ludic ecology will offer the possibility of new or diverse or pleasurable experiences, which will be different for each person. As Meares (1992: 5) tells us: 'The field of play is where, to a large extent, a sense of self is generated'. Building on Gordon and Esbjorn-Hargens (2007), that self could be brought about through environmental exploration, fantasy games, playful heroism, intellectual games, competitive sports, improvisational movement and drama, or by being spontaneous, highly creative, original and open.

The *play frame* is where all this takes place, 'decided' by the playing child. Ultimately all frames are flexible, capable of extending, shrinking or disappearing altogether. However, they create reference points; without the boundary we would not be able to say, 'this is playful, that is not', and children would not be able to define or understand their play content. While children are better at dealing with chaos than most adults, they still need to 'be in control of being out of control' (Gordon and Esbjorn-Hargens 2007), and boundaries and constraints permit that. We should be cautious about our ability to accurately gauge or assess the frame, yet without that examination we would be unable to contribute to the child's play in a way that is truly child-centred. The play frame sits within and influences and is influenced by the ludic ecology.

In summary, the ludic ecology, while itself a metaphorical construct, helps us understand the field of play and the child's place within it. The field or ecology emphasizes that many environmental factors, both physical and psychical, will impact on the child's play; that adults and others are part of the ludic field only adds to the complexity of the interactions. The primary player may be acting instinctively or consciously, in the physical world or in the world of story; others playing with them may be in the same mode or another altogether. Adults in the play space should be careful to respond from a conscious, reflective perspective for fear of leading the children along their own well-worn paths or becoming lost in the space themselves.

With a *ludic consciousness* we might perceive the child's play universe and the meeting with the external world as a flexible, holistic and *ludic* process; this is very different to seeing it as an educational or instructive process. A ludic consciousness helps us see that activities are chosen by the child, not set by the adult; that the child will persevere if they see meaning in the activity and any satisfaction is theirs, based on what they get from the activity. As adults supporting play, by reading the child's encounter with the world and the subsequent response, adaption and adjustment processes, we can contribute to the child's development in a way that is play-centred, child-centred, and encourages the beneficial potentials of play to take effect.

The *ludic process* reflects the interplay of three subjectivities: the subjectivity of the child, of the adult and of the *ludic third* (Sturrock 2003). The ludic third is a creation of the first player and the second player, and at the same time, the players are created by the ludic third (after Ogden's *analytic third* 1994) – that is, what the child wants to play impacts on how the adult responds, and the response will impact upon the child. The resulting *third*, the interaction between the child and the adult, is influenced by each of them and they are influenced by the interaction – i.e. they are likely to behave differently after the interaction than before it, in a way that was not foreseeable. While in most conversations or interactions, the child or adult would act 'naturally' and spontaneously, the adult/worker would be aware of the influence of the ludic third when they are *self-witnessing*.

Self-witnessing is where the worker reflects on their practice from the *witness position* (Kabat-Zinn 1991), the analysis of the self in relation to a relationship with a playing child; it is where the adult is able to mentally 'step back' from the relationship so that they do not become overly involved in the play – they are playing at playing, if need be, but are otherwise outside of the play frame initiated by the child. The aim of *self-witnessing* is for the worker to be their own object of scrutiny.

The *witness position* is where the adult/worker is objectively (impartially) aware of their subjective relationship with another: the playing child. Subjectivity often relies on thoughts and feelings of a personal nature; children will naturally act subjectively in their play. Practitioners need to act objectively (but not authoritatively) in relation to the child's emotional content; workers therefore need to be aware of their own affect (their emotional mood or mask) and the impact of this material on their interactions and relationships with others, especially children. Therefore they need to 'witness' their own behaviour in the play space.

Taking this stance allows the adult to reflect on their behaviour and decide if it was appropriate. When reacting to playing children we may be making very quick decisions and commenting 'off the cuff' – with experience and knowledge these responses are often appropriate and relevant – however, there will be times when we get it wrong. If we do not change our behaviour there is a likelihood that the mistake will be repeated; by paying attention to it, a new behaviour may be substituted to see what the outcome might be.

To add to this learning, *reflection* with a regular review of the work practice of the adult's responses and behaviour should take place both before and after the session. The reflection must examine the themes and material that could not be predicted. Practitioners will form quick judgements about what to do in the play space; after the session, reflection will help with understanding the adult's judgement at that time; this is discussed in Chapter 7.

The *reflective continuum* involves an awareness of both self (Who I am) and self-reflection (How I behave) that goes beyond the mechanistic recording of data – i.e. 'who said what to whom, where'. It is reflection in the moment during the play session, 'reflection-*in*-action' and reflection after the event, 'reflection-*on*-action' in order to become a better practitioner and a better person (after Schön 1983 – discussed in Chapter 7). This awareness is relatively easy for adults to adopt once they become aware of it, and of their impact in the ludic ecology. However, not being aware of it can lead to problems that impinge upon the child's play; these problems include *adulteration* and *contamination*.

Adulteration occurs when the adult dominates or takes over a child's play for their own purposes, whether those purposes are conscious (for example, working to educational or safety standards) or unconscious (fear, embarrassment, domination). When adults want to show children how to 'play the right way' conscious adulteration occurs. In many play settings, the rules of play will have been decided without input from the children; indeed some settings use signs bought from a catalogue. Such signs state things like 'We play well with others – we don't spoil others' games' or 'We are honest – we don't cover up the truth' or 'We care for the playground – we don't damage or spoil anything'. It is easy to see how these rules fit with an adult or society's sense of fairness, justice or respect. Yet many play activities are none of these things; a playground would be a very boring place if all the children played the same game – a possible consequence of not spoiling others' play. Some games demand pretend, covering up the truth or 'lying'. Should we prevent children from pretending to be wolves, or kings and queens, or anything? And where would creativity be without the opportunity to change or manipulate the environment? Many adults are able to make perfectly rational decisions without such unnecessary rules; we should trust their responses and their reflections, rather than a set prescription.

Case Study 5.1 – Philpot 2013

A child at an afterschool club used to have a hard time playing with the other children. *Evan* was 7 years old and attended the same primary school as the majority of children at the afterschool club. A particular practitioner was concerned that each time Evan was invited to play by other children he would display signs of frustration and distress; his behaviour was beginning to make the other children stop asking him, and eventually Evan became isolated and excluded.

The practitioner had a meeting with Evan's father to discuss his play behaviour and it was revealed that, influenced by Evan's short, yet colourful history, he had a tough time taking instruction and direction from others.

With this new information and without adulterating the play, the practitioners made a subtle attempt to support Evan in deciding the nature of the play in group games. They felt that it gave Evan a sense of empowerment and eventually led Evan not only to initiate games with the children, but to join in when asked.

At the setting six months later, Evan was seen playing 'schools' with four or five other children. Evan was the 'teacher' and the other children were the pupils. It appeared that all of the children were enjoying the game. Ten minutes later, Evan had swapped roles with another child and was sitting on the floor taking direction from the new teacher.

Unconscious adulteration happens in part because of *unplayed-out material* – the dormant yet laden play impulses of adults that may manifest in play interchanges with children. Unplayed-out materials are the play desires of adults that were not realized in their own childhood, either though lack of opportunity, fear or adult control. If not recognized and dealt with, unplayed-out material may result in adulteration of the children's play, as the play focus takes on greater meaning for the adult than the child. This can occur in ball games where the adult player forgets to self-limit and kicks or hits a ball at full weight, or when an adult takes over a child's painting and shows a child the 'proper way' to complete a scene or pattern. Becoming aware of our own unplayed-out material, through reflection can lead to us recognizing it and acknowledging it, but not privileging it over the children's play focus. It may result in benefits for both the children and the supporting adult.

Contamination in play occurs when the children's self-chosen play is affected adversely by the actions or comments of others (usually adults). Contamination may occur through concerns about safety, expected compliance with cultural norms, or through an attempt to guide or teach the child how to play or behave. The adult's intentions may be conscious and internally valid, yet will affect the child's play. If the point of play is to stimulate brain connections, explore the physical, social, cultural and cognitive domains, and feel good, then adults 'helping' children is the last thing needed. When visiting pubic playgrounds, it is common to see parents helping their children up the stairs to the slide, or even avoiding the stairs altogether and just sliding down the chute; all the fun and none of the effort. That 'help' denies the child the chance to learn to do it for themselves, 'overcoming obstacles, making their own decisions, developing their own skills, taking their own risks, and coping with their own feelings' (Bassford Baker 2012). Contamination may also lead to 'dysplay' if the child is prevented from or unable to complete the play cycle for themselves.

Dysplay is apparent when children's play cues are laden with anxiety; the cues become urgent, imperative and frantic, usually increasing in speed, force and volume (if spoken). This behaviour in some environments is deemed anti-social or violent, and children may be punished for simply trying to make their views known. When outdoors in many play environments, it is usual to run around, throw things, scream and express emotions exaggeratedly, doing a lot of what is usual for children. However, in some adult-controlled environments where space is limited, where certain cultural values are promoted or where education is being delivered, these behaviours may cause problems for the adults and then the children in those environments. Children denied choice will be inhibited in their play, and the play cycle will be incomplete. The child's play drive will try to compensate with cues that are more urgent or aberrant, resulting in the observable behaviour, dysplay. The correct response to dysplay should not be punishment, but recognition of what the child is trying to communicate so that the play cycle may be completed and the child can respond to the adult's play return in a more usual way. There are many ways that adults can interact or *intervene* in children's play before sanctions become necessary.

The four *levels of intervention* should be *ludocentric* (play-centred) in their intent; the aim of the intervention is to support the play then withdraw as soon as practicable to allow the child free expression and action within their play.

When play is self-contained, children are active in their play, which may be taking many forms and behaviours, no intervention is necessary, the adult/worker observes the activity – this is level 1, *play maintenance*. The adult's role is to ensure that, should children need it, they can offer assistance or support.

Simple involvement is a level 2 intervention; the adult acts as a resource for the play – this may be subtle, as in making a tool available for use that the child may need – e.g. a spade for a sand tray or a hammer for den building – or more overt when responding to a direct request from children. The tool, toy, resource is offered and children continue playing.

Medial intervention describes level 3: at the request of the child, the adult becomes involved in the play – such as by offering alternatives from which the child chooses, or by initiating a game then withdrawing. If the child cannot decide between alternatives, the adult could offer options to help with the decision. If the adult starts a game, be that stacking bricks, a ball game or a chase game, then the aim should be to find another child willing to take the adult's role. Of course it may be that the child simply wants to interact with the adult, to share their day and conversation. The adult should be attuned to the child's affect and be able to read their unspoken wish, though with an awareness that adulteration, the adult taking over the game, should not take place.

The fourth *ludocentric* level is *complex intervention*. In many settings and play spaces, the adult will be interacting with more than one or a few children; there is a need to interact differently and appropriately with them all as needed. This results in *complex interventions*; a direct and extended overlap between the playing children and the adult – the adult may need to simply observe, take on a role in the play, act as a partner to the playing child, or when facing dysplay give a child one-to-one support until the episode passes.

The four levels of intervention should be *ludocentric*, aiming to maintain play. There will, of course, be times when the duty of care requires adults/ workers to behave in a non-ludocentric manner – for example, when a child is in imminent danger of seriously harming themselves or others. Mature judgements on when to make such a *non-ludocentric intervention* will be informed by the adult/worker's level of understanding of their knowledge of the child/ children and the contexts and the adult's instant or dynamic risk assessment, and how the play 'plays through them' as adults. For example, a child playing near a fire pit, who is acting with awareness of the flames, may cause anxiety for the adult but is not a reason for them to intervene. A child jumping over the pit, or recklessly piling on flammable material may not be aware of the potential risks, so a word of caution might be necessary so that the child can still enjoy the fire without being harmed. Many play activities have the potential to awake in the adult fears of embarrassment, physical fear, emotional fear or lack of control; self-witnessing and reflection can help in dealing with these fears.

The *integrity of intervention* is where the adult/worker is aware of any interventions they may need to make in a play session in order to make them as playful as possible; they are aiming to be true to the child's play wish without overburdening it with their own fears or judgements. In a busy setting (or home back garden) the adult may be involved in disputed or conflicting frames as children's play needs overlap and collide – the adult may be called on to make judgements affecting the play frames of several children, or may need to remind a child of the risks taken when crossing boundaries. Where possible, the adult/worker should aim to offer a response that is playful rather than controlling or prescriptive; for example, advising children who wish to play a ball game close to where others are doing chalk drawings to move further down the street or play space.

Though of course if play becomes cruel, hurtful or dangerous, adults will at some point feel compelled to intervene and umpire the situation – such intervention should always be done with an awareness of why we are intervening and what is happening for the child. It may help to think about what would happen if such play took place outside the setting we are in – and if play is 'self-chosen', surely the child has the opportunity to leave the play frame and seek their own play. Bates reminds us that in play children are not subject to a world that is beyond their control but to a world whose conditions of uncertainty are of their own making (Bates 1999: ii). She goes on: 'Children are endlessly inventive in acting out variations on what is, for them, a most uncontrolled and unpredictable existence. If children are subject to a mysterious adult world where the control – if not meaning – of events is often beyond them, they re-assert their power in play' (Bates 1999: 11). This should be reassuring; children will play in most circumstances, though if the conditions become too extreme they may lead to play deprivation, which is discussed below.

The integrity of intervention requires adults to be *authentic*; being honest and open with children and other members of the staff team about how they feel and what their thoughts and feelings are or were in particular situations. Children need to be offered honesty and truthfulness in the responses from the adults around them if they are to best make sense of their world. In one play setting in Wrexham, North Wales (Tawil 2012), the staff and children were well aware that one member of staff enjoyed and was comfortable climbing high and jumping off structures on to small mats below; another member of staff did not feel confident or responsible in that situation. It became normal on the play site that when the one staff member was present extra-high jumping did not take place, but with the other it did. Similar understandings might be needed, for example, with dressing-up, singing or performing, non-traditional activities or culturally challenging activities. Many people have comfort boundaries that they are reluctant to cross; authenticity in practice helps everyone understand what those are. Authenticity helps adults be in service to children when they play; this is necessary for containment when working with playing children.

The support that adults/workers can give to children in play should include the ability to hold or *contain* the play. *Containment* is about supporting a child through their initial play cues, giving back a return to help the play on its way. It may also be about holding the frame while the child is away from the play (or when the play ends for the day). Two children were playing in a nursery, taking it in turns to pull each other in a wooden truck along a track; suddenly the pulling child started hopping around on his toes, as a sign that he wanted to go to the toilet. A practitioner, noticing his distress, went across and took hold of the truck handle, as which point the boy ran off to the toilet. His partner sat quietly in the truck waiting for the other to return, neither the adult nor the passenger said anything for the two minutes it took the first boy to return. When he did, he took over the handle of the truck from the adult and the play continued. In more general play, it may be that the adult notices that mealtime is approaching or the setting is about to close. A careful practitioner would give the children clues that the session was about to end and would make a note of where the play had got to for the day, to help the children resume the next day (some settings use digital cameras to record the position of items so that they may be laid out the same way the following day).

Additionally, our professional containment is a crucial element of working practice, knowing where boundaries are between play and non-play, between the adult and the child, between what is playful and what harmful. Without an understanding of boundaries and when to hold or contain them, adults working with playing children may drift into adulteration or contamination all too easily. Understanding boundaries and the playing child will help adults with *translation* and *transformation*.

Translation is a term defined by Wilber (1980) to indicate those states of experience where the self is simply given a new way to think or feel about reality, but which ultimately does not lead to transformation or change. For example, no matter how much individuals play with 'world making' games such as *Sim City*, the game cannot fully equip them for life in the real world, using real tools, relating to real people. The more successful an individual becomes at a given sport, it does not indicate that they will become more tolerant of others or self-reflective. Children (and many adults) can be seen obsessively collecting more and more things to play with, yet that does not guarantee play will change or offer more satisfaction. An example would be an 'aggressive player' (Gordon and Esbjorn-Hargens 2007), where the play involves war games, play-fighting, symbolic acts of heroism, then later the risk game 'chicken', as adults drinking games or real fighting. The form of play has not really changed, it has just translated to become more extreme. A change in the play would be to move into sensitive play – understanding the needs of another player – or complex play where others are accepted despite any perceived negative traits.

Generally read as 'change or alteration', *transformation* is to rise above or exceed a prior form or state of oneself (Wilber 1980). In play, children may outdo previous levels of experience, in each of the four realms of self, physical body, cultural and social relationships. In transformation, new skills and/ or knowledge are acquired that could not have occurred beforehand, yet with the retention of the previous knowledge or state of experience. For example, when children learn to walk they are still able to crawl, when they learn to relate to strangers, they can still relate to family members and friends. Transformation occurs during normal play and growth when children have access to a variety of play opportunities that offer balance in activities, feeling thoughts and actions without play deprivation adversely affecting the child; transformation may also occur during peak experiences, when an individual exceeds themselves through chance or by pushing through with a new activity.

Children (like adults) are capable of *peak experiences* that add to their knowledge and feelings about the world. Peak experiences (after Maslow 1964) are especially joyous and exciting moments in life, involving sudden feelings of intense happiness and well-being, wonder and awe. In play children may often have experiences that offer such feelings, however it may be many years before they are able to integrate the skills and knowledge necessary to replicate those moments at will. A moment of deep play may help children feel connected to all things and aware of their mortality, a state they may not fully feel again until older and nearer to death. Role Play may be carried out with the intensity of a Shakespearean actor during a playground production, yet not be replicated later due to growing awareness of an audience or fear of failure.

So how can adults help?

Play occurs when a child (or other human) wants to play; it requires a space in which to play but does not require another player, or an adult to supervise or guide the play. Yet another player can support or add to the play, just as can the playwork practitioner or other sensitive adult. First and foremost, especially when children are playing in supervised settings, play-sensitive adults give support or permission for the play to continue. At first when using settings, children may be concerned about what is allowed – can they borrow equipment, dare they take things outside, how high can they climb? Each setting has rules (written or assumed) about expected behaviour that children quickly pick up when adults are overly domineering, controlling or aggressive. Adults should epitomize good behaviour in settings and be enthusiastic in their support of play. Adults working with children in their play should be possessed with the divine spirit of playfulness, not to play for themselves but so that they can interact with children in a spirit of playfulness.

If children seek help or advice, the adult can make offers or invitations to play, either subtly through play cues or more obviously through direct comment or action. The aim should always be to withdraw to leave children to expand their own play in whatever way they want, but occasionally a worker will be called on to provide resources, spaces or make adaptations to help play go on. Adults working with children in their play will need an open attitude; being judgemental has no place near children's play – at times children will be loud, destructive, argumentative and confrontational in their play with other children. If the adult steps in too quickly, the child will not be able to work out for themselves what to do, they will end up always turning to the adult to help them with problems they may face. Sorting things out for themselves helps children develop resilience to cope with stress (Burghardt 2005); adults cannot do that for children.

As we saw earlier (Figure 4.1 – Integral Play Framework and spaces for play), when interacting with children there are three main ways that adults can work with them: face to face with children in the setting; in the background managing and organizing the spaces; and by advocating for play at governmental and national levels.

Interacting with children: face-to-face work

Practitioners who work daily with children should support and facilitate the play process (this assumes a working knowledge of the process), the self-chosen activities that children take part in when playing. Adults who work face to face with children should support the essential characteristics of play and the need for play in the wider community. These are the aptitudes the practitioner should have:

- an open attitude of curiosity to the child's play, waits to see what emerges and engages or not with that play activity; they are enthusiastic, make invitations and give permission when needed
- supports sufficient physical and psychological safety for the player, so that the individual feels accepted and free to do as they wish within the play space
- a provider/enabler of a variety of spaces for children to play, with varied resources and challenges that change frequently
- 'cultural competence' – of their own and others' cultures
- skilled in sensitive assessments of the children's play cues, pays attention to the player and, through the awareness developed, offers a response/variety of responses to support the play, aiming to intervene as little as possible unless requested/needed by the child
- integrity and authenticity (and so a degree of self-knowledge), supporting the play while being aware of their own influence on it and/or their possible response to it
- an up-to-date knowledge base including child development and the influences on childhood
- has a willingness to take risks, be creative, adapt, reflect often on their work and aim to improve their practice
- understands the value and benefits of play, and is an advocate for the right to play for the child

- understands that engagement in play is the child's choice and cannot be forced or prolonged
- understands that external evaluation should be absent in the play space, and that satisfaction and any outcomes from the play are the child's
- has a sense of humour!

Again, children do not need adults in order to play, yet adults can support play through the provision of play spaces and opportunities that may never occur otherwise.

Case Study 5.2 – Philpot 2013

At a holiday camp for children with additional needs, the staff were told by the parents of Mia (13) that she 'did not know how to play'. Not only that but staff were told she could not do anything for herself; Mia had spina bifida and cerebral palsy, and was mute.

With regards to play, the camp aimed to be child-centred and had limited structure to the programme. Her key carer, a worker, would ask Mia where she wanted to go and what she wanted to do. As Mia could not speak directly, the worker would walk Mia around the activities and the other children until her eyes or her hands suggested she wanted to stop.

On one particular day, some of the children set up a game involving throwing wet sponges at the opposing team. When Mia and the worker approached this game, her eyes blinked and her hand moved up and down. The worker asked Mia if she wanted to join in, in response she continued her eye and hand movement. One of the children placed a wet sponge in Mia's hand and another child helped lift her hand to throw the sponge at the opposite team. The worker walked away from the game and observed. Eventually, the majority of the children were helping Mia play the game, by placing sponges in her hand and running slower so she could hit them. Mia then began to laugh, a lot!

Vygotsky (1976) wrote about the social role of other children and adults in the child's play and life; how having more experienced others nearby helped the individual do more and go further than they had done before. Konner (2010), writing about mother–infant interactions, reports that mothers with an 'intermediate' level of synchrony (match) to their baby's vocalizations were more helpful than those who were very like or very unlike their children:

> intermediate stimulus patterns are a source of pleasure, which is enhanced by a certain degree of control. This is the zone of play, and the most sensitive parents lead infants into it. However, because adaptation

level changes with long-term stimulation, the amount and type of stimulation that will produce optimal arousal also change – a key process in development.

Konner (2010: 505)

Konner is arguing that infant children are not attracted to or stimulated by the 'easy' modes of communication, nor by the very hard ones; they like the ones that are 'just right'. This approach seems to work just as well with older children for whom the 'intermediate stimulus' – neither too hard nor too easy – is what is needed to stimulate and satisfy them.

This idea is supported by the work of Csikszentmihalyi (1990), who coined the term *flow* after studying when and where people were 'happiest' or had *optimal experiences*. People in flow were experiencing something that was not too easy but was challenging and therefore stimulating; it usually involved a combination of mind and body working together, and it was informed by immediate feedback from the environment and those in it:

> The best moments usually occur when a person's body or mind is stretched to its limits in a voluntary effort to accomplish something difficult and worthwhile. Optimal experience is thus something that we *make* happen. For a child, it could be placing with trembling fingers the last block on a tower she has built; for a swimmer, it could be trying to beat his own record; for a violinist, mastering an intricate musical passage.
>
> *Csikszentmihalyi (1990: 3, original emphasis)*

Csikszentmihalyi notes that children and other individuals make this experience for themselves. In free play, where children are playing in the street, on the beach or in wild places with no adults present, the play may be considered fully child-led and they will be in full control (within the limits of human action) of the activity and experience. In many places in children's lives, adults will be present, not least in school and in play provision; at such times adults may try to lead the activities. We should also be aware of the words of Eloise Green (aged 10¾, 2012), 'Play in school is work in disguise', which is what happens when play becomes too adult led.

In general practice, play activities will be a balance between these two extremes – this point was noted by Russell (2005). Table 5.1 illustrates the extremes of this adult-led/child-led continuum, and that a balanced approach may be the better way of supporting playing. Of course no one setting or experience can be fully described using this tool – the issues are too complex and affected by context and the players in the space – yet the dialogue that emerges from discussing such issues will be useful to practice and the support of playing children.

Table 5.1 A comparison of child-led playing with adult-led approaches.

Adult led	Balanced – playing together	Child led
Adult controlled – limited choice may be given to the child	**Child choice/involvement Adult supports**	Child controlled – freedom of choice
Adult solely responsible	**Joint responsibility**	Child solely responsible
Follows a curriculum/controlled	**Thematic, ideas emerge**	Flexible/things emerge randomly
Designed for the future, i.e. skills for adulthood, health and well-being	**Balanced, enjoyable and focused on benefits, e.g. education or therapeutic**	In the moment i.e. for pleasure, expressive
Works to expected standards and outcomes – extrinsic	**Adults 'scaffold' the child's experiences** **The involvement of adults and more experienced peers (other children) makes a difference in the playing process**	Follows the child's interests – fundamental
Playing activities are planned	**Playing follows negotiated interests**	Play led – playing happens by accident
Resources may be planned for the programme	**Creative, working with existing resources**	Resources may not be available
Controlled attitude to safety	**Risk benefits assessed with the aim of balancing risk and challenge**	May be risky

While adults who work with children are aware of some of these issues, other things can take precedence or get in the way. In May 2011, 45 playwork, care and education practitioners in Penicuik, Scotland, were asked about the role of adults in play. Their comments were analysed using the Integral Play Framework and, like the *elements for play provision* shown in Table 4.4, there was a major focus on the observable, physical and social elements.

The playwork, care and education practitioners said that 'facilitating play' was their main focus, 'putting things out – materials, but also creating spaces, and using their own knowledge of play'. They said that observation was important to challenge the children's expectations but without 'helping too much' – in a good environment (especially outdoor ones) they 'stood back' to let the children get on with it.

They stated that there was 'too much paperwork', that inspection regimes got in the way of their 'real work', and that legislation and policies were too detached from face-to-face work. The practitioners recognized that safety and rules were important, and that 'No rules = mayhem', but they wanted to talk to and negotiate with the children to agree what was necessary. They knew that risk and challenge should be part of the play experience but that risk constantly changed, and that fact ought to be considered when carrying out the required risk assessments.

Culturally, the practitioners recognized that 'Play depended on the context' and that different parenting approaches affected children in many ways. One of these was time, which they saw as being controlled by parents, who had the choice of when children could arrive at the setting and when they must leave. Another issue was described as 'Nasty play' – was it playful? Could children 'go too far' and who decided? They also raised the question of 'Whose values' should dominate in the setting; the children's, the parents' or the staff's?

Finally while the workers recognized that play should be free and child-led, they were aware of their own 'Unplayed-out material, our play needs' and how they could affect staff confidence in responding to the children's needs and desires.

Some of these issues are addressed by the UK Playwork Principles (PPSG 2005), which aim to set the parameters for playwork practice, and say that the play process should take precedence and playworkers must act as advocates for play when engaging with 'adult-led agendas'. Practitioners should support all children and young people in the creation of a space in which to play. They should have a sound, up-to-date knowledge of the play process, and should be reflective practitioners. Playworkers should recognize their own impact on the play space and children, and playwork intervention must balance risk with the developmental benefit and well-being of children. These are laudable principles to aspire to in face-to-face work, but they are often not supported by those in control of provision, for example in management or funding positions.

Interacting with children is a complex business; it can be carried out quite 'naturally' when adults feel an activity is crossing some rule of their own, but to get closer to understanding the play exchange there are several elements to consider – the play cycle, psycholudics and the Integral Play Framework can help with those elements at the face-to-face level. In the final analysis, adults may influence and affect children's play only when they are in the same space. Much play happens every day and away from the view of well-meaning adults or carers. Adults may find these forms of play threatening or frightening, but we need to understand that, when playing, children control a world where the conditions of uncertainty and challenge are of their own making.

Questions to help practitioners interact with children using the play cycle

- Make sure you understand five of the features of the play cycle; watch a group of children playing and tick off when you see the features appearing in their play. What happens between the children? How often do the cues change? How often do the activities change? Who initiated the change; was it always the same person?
- Thinking about adulteration and containment, start looking for examples of it in your daily life – how often do adults tell children what to do? Are the interventions justified? Would you have reacted the same way? If not, what would be different?
- Looking at Table 5.1 – *A comparison of child-led playing with adult-led approaches* – what is your approach to children? Where would you put yourself on the table? Are you willing to try a different approach to working with playing children? Could you give up a little of your power to let them make more decisions and choices?

6

What kids get up to: everydayness and the darker side of play

Often when describing children's play, writers tend to emphasize the ideal states of play for the child and the environment. Yet quite frequently in their spontaneous play children are not in ideal states or conditions – things just happen, they react to the playfulness of a space or they play in ways that others consider to be inappropriate. In playing with feelings and identity children will often display anger as well as enjoyment, the latter of which is better valued by many adults. Yet enjoyment can also result in hedonism, which is frowned on by a puritanical work ethic. In play children are often fascinated by strangeness, despite 'strangers' being social pariahs in the west. How do children find a way through these contradictions? This chapter will explore these ways of playing, looking at the individual and cultural aspects of play as well as its physical and social manifestations. The issues of play deprivation and 'deep play' (Hughes 2002) will be explored.

Everydayness of play

Play is present in all aspects of life; in conversations, observations, daydreams, thoughts, interactions and experiments. Play can emerge for microseconds or last for days; a playful moment can break into an otherwise dull day and lighten everyone's faces, or it may be a state of mind that lasts a lifetime. Play is there 'everyday'; it needs no special label to say 'this is play' (though many people will recognize it when it happens) nor does it need a special place to happen. Play can be commonplace and repetitive, it can be ordinary. Can it be mundane and monotonous? Probably not, that is its *magic*. As Stuart Lester put it, 'Play is not something that is set apart from the real world but draws on and disturbs everyday practices' (Lester 2010: 3). Every day, play challenges the status quo, challenges expectations of normalness and 'good behaviour' – play goes on all around us; it is a biological, behavioural and cognitive drive, it will happen because that is what children need to do, it is what evolution has equipped them to do. In spite of this, playing continues to be misunderstood, misused and misrepresented. Hughes reminds us that, 'Play is not always the pleasant experience some would have us believe. It can be chaotic, it can be physically painful, it can contain rejection, it can also contain fear and panic (Hughes 2006: 22–23). One of the ways children find to play every day is by breaking rules.

Following the rules

It was Bronfenbrenner (1979) who first noted that many of the theories about children's behaviour were based on un-lifelike experiments, in strange places conducted for brief moments of a child's life. To address this disconnection from reality he developed his Ecological Systems Theory (1979) locating children at the centre of their life-worlds, always affecting and being affected by the surrounding environment and the people in it. Children have to be understood (as best as we are able) within the worlds they inhabit – whether those worlds are challenging, comfortable, Muslim, Christian, Atheist, Asian, European, American, dirty or clean, rich or poor. As Grieshaber and McArdle (2010: 29) stated, 'The trouble with the idea that play is children's natural way of learning is that ideas about what is natural in children are selective. They are a conglomeration of science, tradition, history, culture, and other ideas. And they vary across time and place'. Some modes of play will be affected by what is happening in those worlds; when a 6-year-old child states to a play-mate, 'I know the rules – I am a Muslim/I am a Catholic', etc., is that a fully conscious thought or a learned reaction?

Children need to break rules to find out the edge of the frame physically, psychically, socially and culturally, making everyday magic – 'That gap looks big, can I jump it?', 'Those people are wrong, can I challenge them?' – they need to play with the people, situations and the things they find. Without exploring, challenging and mastering the world around them, they are not likely to be fully conscious nor can they truly understand how it all works. Children experience things then make sense of them as best they can in their heads; 'Playing is a very serious activity that is part of our survival mechanism in the human world' (Jennings 1995: 140). Playing allows children to make sense of what is pretend and what is real life (as far as it may be known). This exploring is not scientific, it happens when it happens and in surprising ways. As a society we tend to look at things in a binary manner – in terms of black and white, yes and no, past and future – but reality is more complex than that.

A 'simple' game like 'tig/tag/it' may involve many different aspects of the child's world (challenge, confidence, culture and community); while princi-pally a locomotor-based game (everyone is running about) the person who is 'on', and so leading the game, changes every few minutes. Doing well in the game, catching or avoiding others, can lead to a feeling of well-being (unless it's too easy or too hard), and often creates bonding between some or all members of the group. This type of game is frequently played between friends and a known group of friends rather than strangers, as it is easier to negotiate the rules and 'play fair'. Children will quickly let others know if things are not fair, whether by challenging their behaviour or voting with their feet and walking away.

Sometimes children stay in the others' game and play a part rather than play the game; other times they join in the game, and then again they may leave the game. Flemmen (2005) calls this the 'pre-school of democracy': one child tries to assert their authority by trying to set the rules of the game; the other child refuses to play as it feels 'unfair'. The first child offers an alternative, the second offers a compromise and the first says, 'OK then' and the play cycle is formed – or not, if the compromise is unacceptable and a child walks away. As Brian Sutton-Smith (1997: 173) put it, 'Play is intrinsically motivated . . . except if you don't do what the others tell you, they won't let you play.' So rules are useful some of the time but they do not constrain or control play; if anything they become another thing to play with as the child attempts to make sense of the social world they inhabit.

In society there are many rules that affect children playing, from the obvious, 'Keep off the grass' to the manipulative, 'You can go outside when you have finished your tea/homework/chores' – permission is given, but at a price. Numerous rules apply in many situations: the home, the friend's home, the street, the park, the school, the afterschool club, the religious centre, the medical centre, the art gallery. Children can 'be themselves' in some places, and need to 'behave' in others; in some they have to do what adults tell them or they'll get into trouble. It's no wonder that children get confused trying to remember what is 'allowed' where. This results in two opposing responses in children that reflect the expectations and judgements of society: 'The over-protected child assumes there must be terrifying things out there if he needs so much protection and lives in fear' (Phillips 2005: 61), yet in order to become autonomous, self-governing individuals, children need to do things for themselves, make choices (and mistakes), and step outside the limits and rules imposed by adults just to see what happens; and this can bring them into trouble with those in authority.

I don't know about your kids, but the first word each of mine mastered was 'No'. The same was true for me as a kid, and probably for you as well. From the corrective ('No, you can't have cake for dinner') to the protective ('No! Johnny, never pee in the wall socket'), 'No' is how we establish and begin to comprehend boundaries.

But this doesn't mean 'No' is only about limits. By giving a child the means with which to define his or her own unique identity and sense of self, pronouncing the word 'No' marks the first step on the road to autonomy.

Michael J. Fox (2002: 106)

Through play, children experience their world and relationships within it . . . yet adults sometimes like to describe the play as 'good' or 'bad', and particularly in settings where children are encouraged to play, the rules can be quite odd. The following are some of the rules that may be found on school playground walls:

- Keep your hands and feet to yourself
- Say nice things to other people
- Never swear in the school grounds
- Be a good friend; let other people join in your games
- Ask an adult to sort out any difficulties
- Be sensible in all areas
- When you play a game stick to the rules

If children followed these rules to the letter there could be no games of tag, no hand holding, no hugs and celebrations. Children grow up in a world where they hear terrible things said in the street, on the TV and sometimes from one adult to another, but they are expected to be 'nice to others' and not swear. Part of socialization is finding out who is a friend and who not, who's in the gang and who outside; understanding the boundaries is a key part of becoming human, so to be told to play with everyone can be quite confusing. Asking adults to sort out problems takes power and choice away from the children; they will not learn how to sort things out for themselves for what they may face in life. 'Being sensible' is such an adult term; how many children know what it means these days? It's a bit like being asked to 'use your common sense'; when children have such diverse backgrounds and cultures, what is sensible in one culture may be considered impractical in another. And as was discussed above, playing is often about playing with the rules, negotiating and finding new ways of doing things.

'Rules are one way in which adults are able to adopt positions of power in relation to children,' say Grieshaber and McArdle (2010: 60), and it is not just in children's settings. At home the rules can be just as well-meaning but just as unreal. The website *Parenting by the Minute* (2010) has a parent worried that, 'Disney taught my kids bad words' – the bad words in question were 'stupid' and 'kill you' taken from the Disney/Pixar movie *A Bug's Life* (1998). The parent's response was to deny 'a toy or TV privileges until they were ready to practice choosing better words'. Another parent (on *Momlogic* 2009) was concerned that 'My kid's a liar'. While the advice offered was sensible, that all children will lie at different times in their childhood, the parent's concerns showed a desire to bring their child up in an ideal world that cannot exist. Nor are these examples isolated; a case in the USA involved a mother who felt that *The Diary of Anne Frank* was too pornographic for her 12-year old daughter and wanted it to be removed from the school reading list (Huffington Post 2013); and, in the UK, when young children were given warning letters from police officers for playing outside (Metro 2013), other parents were keen to state how responsible they were for keeping their own children in the house and garden where they could be supervised.

Rules are important and are part of the social glue that makes modern societies work. Yet children will want to play with them just as they do all other aspects of their lives, and if they cannot do it at home, in school or other children's settings, they will do it in the street and playground. Adults should be aware of the levels of comprehension and maturity in children when they try to impose adult expectations of behaviour on young people.

Everyday ways of playing

For every form of playing there is a continuum of behaviour from 'acceptable' to 'unacceptable'. The value of acceptance will vary from person to person and place to place; who is it that decides what is acceptable? In the home it will be the parent, in school the teacher, in the street the neighbour. But what if children are away from adult scrutiny, what happens then? We have already looked at the forms of play and mapped them to the Integral Play Framework (Figure 3.2), but what are the social limits of those forms of play and the murkiest corners of all – being left out of the game, being picked on, exploring sexuality, exploring sexual difference and deviance – do these have a place in 'good' play?

Looking at emotion and cognition, many people recognize that play helps children feel, particularly positive emotions like pleasure, satisfaction and fun, but what about frustration or anger when things do not go as planned? Is that welcomed or tolerated in society? Sometimes when playing children persevere with an action, and that perseverance is what gives them a breakthrough moment; without the frustration they may never have got there. Stories are important for children, they are often how children learn to understand metaphor and how ideas can mean two things at the same time, or that a word or sound can represent something in the objective world. Stories may often be nonsensical (from the adult's point of view), yet children can be fascinated by them for hours. Yet if the stories stray into talking about bodily functions or unusual fantasies, they may be censored or stopped by well-meaning adults. As Peter and Iona Opie found many years ago (1959), children love making rhymes about rude things. In 2005, David Rowan followed up their work on playground rhymes and songs and found that they were as alive as ever, just updated to modern references. Here are a few of the 'more acceptable' varieties from Rowan (2005):

> Jingle bells, jingle bells, Santa's lying dead.
> Teletubbies Teletubbies stabbed him in his head.
> Barbie girl, Barbie girl tried to save his life.
> Action Man, Action Man stabbed him wi' a knife . . .
>
> *11 year olds, Glasgow*

> Jingle bells, Batman smells,
> Robin flew away.
> Uncle Billy sold his willy for a Milky Way.
>
> *10 year olds, Keighley, West Yorkshire*

> Tweet tweet tweet, on the way we go,
> Walking in the city all day long.
> Mama's in the kitchen, cooking rice chicken.
> Daddy's in the loo, doing number two.
> All the girls in Bombay Stores say the same thing.
> Tweet tweet tweet . . .
>
> *9-year-old girls, Bradford*

In just these three examples we have classic cultural references (Santa and *Jingle Bells*, twice), modern themes (Teletubbies™, Barbie™, Action Man™, Batman™), murder, and allusions to genital organs and bodily functions. Rowan reports that, as these were recorded, the children were aware of how rude they were but still enjoyed playing repeatedly with the rhymes. What richness may be lost if these activities were censored by those uncomfortable with the themes? By playing with these themes, as well as having fun, children find out what is acceptable for them and others, rather than suppressing and shutting off such thoughts. As these examples show, children will play with the themes of their experience, and if those experiences are dark and 'uncomfortable' that is what emerges in their everyday play. Indeed as Holland (2003) says specifically about boys and rough and tumble games, it can be unhelpful to try to stop them playing aggressive and violent games as the feelings can be displaced into 'bad behaviour' as they seek attention in other ways. Playing through the emotion seems to help children come to deal with it in their own way.

When playing physically and moving through the world, there are many forms of play where children like to feel the thrill of being alive. Toddlers enjoy the ecstasy of the swing, shouting 'Higher, higher!' to the parent pushing them. That same thrill leads to climbing higher, riding faster and, eventually, to bungee jumping, street running, or *parkour*, and other extreme sports – often without any safety equipment or crash mats. Sadly in our society children are too often 'banned' from troublesome play that's even slightly challenging in the street, but also in provision because 'It's too risky for staff, in that play could get out of control and children might be hurt' (Grieshaber and McArdle 2010: 61).

And what about feeling extreme pleasure, the ecstasy that children may achieve through particularly intense forms of play, usually physical? The thrill of surprise or achievement is often welcomed and celebrated, yet children of all ages will explore their bodies and emerging sexuality through play, frequently in secret or private places, finding out how things feel and how they work. Grieshaber and McArdle (2010) comment about these matters, saying that many worries about such feelings in the UK and USA go back many centuries, to the Christian concept of *original sin* that has influenced the thinking of writers and parents since at least the seventeenth century. Freedom was constrained and controlled by physical punishment, discipline and strict routines to rid children of 'evil habits'; by playing orderly games and following instruction, children learned the 'right thing' to do (Grieshaber and McArdle 2010). Is it any wonder that many children chose to play in clandestine and covert spaces away from the adult gaze?

These approaches spill over into social roles in play for children where in play it might be quite usual for children to 'borrow' from others without permission, perhaps even stealing or shoplifting as they get older (around 25 per cent of shoplifting is done by children – NASP 2006). For many children the excitement and thrill of the activity is what motivates them, not the items themselves; the thefts are often items such as chewing gum or small bags of sweets (which may be seen as quite trivial in some countries). But as well as being thrilling the activities help children with understanding emotional regulation and deferred gratification, hiding their true emotions in order to get away with the deceit, but also finding out that getting what you want right now is not always the best in the long run. Many of these activities are children playing with the boundaries of social life and what is accepted and tolerated in the community they live in. They understand that some activities, such as making friends, learning to communicate with a variety of people, accommodating others, working in groups and on team activities, are socially accepted ways of relating, but that others are frowned upon or attract penalties from others. It can be confusing for children to know that they are expected not to lie, yet learn about white lies and pretending so as not to hurt people.

As well as fibbing, pretending and shoplifting, which will have different values according to the culture children are born into, some traditions will leave children who 'do not fit' to experience sadness and overcome it in their own way – 'a child is learning on their own', as the indigenous Sami of Finland say about their children coping with self-control (Griffiths 2013); other customs may expect all to be included and to conform to the shared event. Mainstream theories of child development have helped people understand that children will play alone, then copy others, playing in parallel, before cooperating with others – through drama, music, imaginary games. But what if imagination and drama turn into less acceptable actions like 'acting out' or cheating or out-and-out fraud? When was the line crossed? Yet children navigate this territory every day as they go about their lives, playing when and where they can, acting independently, and finding the boundary between rebelling and respecting beliefs. And, again, we should be aware of how different cultures view these activities (thefts even by children can still result in very severe penalties such as mutilation in some countries). In Iran at the start of spring each year (21 March) children participate in fire jumping, leaping over a lit fire to bless the year and take away the bad luck. After jumping over the fire, children usually go door to door in their neighbourhood, making noise by banging on pots with spoons – very similar to what was the UK tradition of Halloween and Mischief Night before they were commercialized and moderated into trick-or-treating.

Looking now at primarily physical play, we can recognize the many ways that children will play with and use their bodies, exploring using their senses, running, jumping, testing their strength, movement, speed, balance, using delicate and coordinating actions, taking control over themselves and their environment, gaining mastery over it in some cases. But in play these things are repeatedly taken 'too far' in the day-by-day experiences of children; exploring dark places and scaring themselves and others, setting up situations where others are scared for fun, testing their bodies to the limit away from the gaze of adult control.

Sometimes the continuum of behaviour from 'acceptable' to 'unacceptable' can be inverted, especially in special places like adventure playgrounds or theatre projects where what others consider unusual behaviour becomes normal; where adults are aware of the benefits of freedom for the child, and encourage that to flourish. Sometimes children do it anyway, whatever environment they are in, for the thrill of challenging the rules and getting away with it without being caught. We should remember that for much of human history, and in much of the world even today, when the majority of children played freely they did so outdoors, doing what they wanted without adults overseeing or guiding that play, taking the episode as far as they felt comfortable. Children still need and seek out these experiences. Even in built-up environments children find everyday play in the spaces between one adult-dominated environment and another, and between one adult-controlled experience and another. With our new awareness of the importance of play experiences in children's lives, we ought to do better by them; we ought to be making community spaces and environments more open to children, not in an attempt to control that play (we would fail) but to help children's natural play drive to emerge.

Deep play

Many of the examples given above could be grouped together and categorized as 'deep play', which Hughes (1996a) initially described as 'risky or even potentially life threatening experiences to develop survival skills and conquer fear'. Hughes' examples focused on physical experiences, such as taking risks with heights, roads, trains and rivers; he later (2006) recognized that this form of play also helped children face issues of death and sex, and awe at the immensity of the universe. Other writers use the term to mean involving or immersive play, where the child cannot easily be distracted from their play, but this interpretation misses some of the qualities that children may experience in deep play.

The Integral Play Framework helps us take this interpretation further and see that risky play, or indeed existential play, may be encountered in each of the four quadrants; physically with heights, depths and bodily explorations, but also socially when children play with new roles and relationships, culturally when they challenge customs and beliefs, and cognitively when they ponder on the immensity of things and the 'meaning of life'. Deep play offers the risk of being hurt physically and emotionally from a variety of sources; the children scaring themselves with shadows in the dark, crawling though drainage ditches, running past 'haunted houses' or balancing on high structures, playing 'chicken' near fast-moving objects, or by throwing knives or darts. They may also be hurt by others wrestling and fighting with them, 'egging them on' to do things the children know are risky, or being tested or 'hazed' prior to acceptance in a gang or clique. And while boys tend to play-fight there is some evidence that girls manipulate others socially through backbiting, gossiping and other forms of manipulation (Bjorkqvist et al. 1991), which is being supported by increasing reports of children of both genders being picked on and 'cyber-bullied' though mobile/ cell phones (Campbell 2007). Technology has also added a new dimension to sexual exploration, with the use of instant photos and hand-held video recorders able to capture intimate details and activities that in previous generations would have taken place in more private places. In previous generations it was usual for children to range far and wide from home; Bird's report (2007) highlighted the comparative loss of freedom for modern children. The differences were highlighted in media reports that showed the changes from 1919–2007 in one family, where a great-grandparent in 1919 was able to roam across a whole city up to 10 km from home, a grandfather 1.6 km, his daughter 0.8 km and, by 2007, her son only 275 m. Anecdotal auto-biographies such as *Cider with Rosie* (Lee 1959), and even fictional stories like *Swallows and Amazons* (Ransome 1930), meanwhile, showed something of what children got up to away from adult control in the early part of the twentieth century.

While many adults do not like to recognize these aspects of children's lives, they are there almost every day and will find a way of coming out. An activity that became popular in the UK post-2000, tombstoning (jumping feet-first off cliffs into the sea in relatively shallow water), as well climbing and bicycling/BMX, can be dangerous activities if not entered into with an awareness of heights and obstacles. Some forms of adolescent and young adult play come very close to being life-threatening forms of play; street running, or *parkour*, bungee jumping, wing-suit sky diving and similar activities all have their annual fatalities. Children and young people have this desire to develop skills in extreme situations and conquer fear.

Carl Jung (1938) argued that all of us have a *shadow side* to our personalities, an unconscious, instinctive aspect of the personality, which the conscious self does not recognize, the feelings and thoughts that we suppress for fear of hurting others or ourselves. The significance of this may be explained by the work of Brown (2009: 89) who, after studying adults convicted of murder in North America, reported that many of them had little experience of rough and tumble play in their early years when compared to adults with similar backgrounds. It was as if by not playing with those feelings in childhood they were suppressed until they burst out catastrophically later in life. Jung stated that unless the shadow was recognized and integrated into the full personality there was a danger that it could take over; 'deep play is a journey into the shadow with every intention of surviving' (Hughes 2006: 41), though sadly a few children do cross the boundary and do not come back. Deep play is one of the opportunities that children need to experience in the world for themselves and, by coming into contact with it, they develop resilience, an essential life skill.

Play and resilience

All children are resilient by nature; they have to be – growing up they face many challenges, both psychologically and physically, and they become hardy, flexible and able to bounce back from whatever happens. From birth children slowly realize they are not the centre of the universe and need to adapt to the world they find themselves in; the physical scars are easy to see, the mental ones a little less visible. Children will be resilient in different ways, most will cope well with some environmental challenges, but not everything they face – think about children who are good/bad with heights, and those curious about dark passages that others would keep well away from. Children will also have different responses to challenges involving other people, some adapting and coping with new situations, others not, and of course this will change during life; the ability to bounce back in response to a threat can be weakened by illness or stress (after Rutter 2006).

As reported by Lester and Russell (2008), research across a number of disciplines shows that play helps the development of resilience across a variety of interrelated adaptive systems – the links between brain and body that may adapt their responses according to changes in the environment, or in parts of the system itself. Play helps build resilience in areas such as emotional regulation, the promotion of positive feelings, stress response systems and the ability to respond to uncertainty, creativity, learning and attachments to people or places (after Lester and Russell 2008: 50).

Emotional regulation is about developing variability and flexibility, and helps with emotional health through pleasure and enjoyment, and so mental and physical health; play helps by rehearsing a wide range of emotions that are varied and regulated within the relatively safe context in which play occurs (Lester and Russell 2008: 52).

The promotion of positive feelings may occur for varied reasons and helps children deal with adversity and ill health – according to Duckworth *et al.* (2005: 635, quoted in Lester and Russell 2008: 62), feeling good or being happy has three interconnected elements: positive emotion about the past (contentment, satisfaction and serenity); bodily pleasures (sensory delights); and 'complex pleasures' (learning and discovery – *wow!*) in the moment, and feeling good about the future (optimism, hope and faith). Together Duckworth *et al.* state that these create a 'pleasant life' that 'maximizes positive emotions and minimizes pain and negative emotion' (Lester and Russell 2008: 62).

Much of children's play involves elements of risk as they seek out new experiences and explore uncertain situations, climbing higher, ranging further and seeking new solutions. Each of these experiences will be mildly risky, raising levels of adrenalin and increasing heart beats, yet will be thrilling and exciting as children come to terms with the challenge and uncertainty they face. Children's response to stress helps them deal with the pressures of the world and equips them for bigger challenges later in life. Indeed some researchers (Siviy 1998; Panksepp 2001; Yun *et al.* 2005) suggest that moderate stress is necessary to exercise and strengthen both neuronal and muscular systems; it is analogous to a daily workout at the gym that keeps the body and brain fit and flexible.

Bateson and Martin (2013: 123) argue that play 'equips the individual with experiences that enable it to meet future challenges in novel ways', and that 'playful thought and playful behaviour can assist creativity and hence help individuals and organisations be more innovative' (2013: 124). Other evidence shows that play can help with flexibility in both mental and physical structures, helping with the development of creative and problem-solving approaches. The links between children's play and adult creativity have long been argued by Jung, Malaguzzi, Robinson and Winnicott, among others, and will be explored in more detail in a later section.

Positive attachments to people or places help with creating an internal sense of security and resilience; if the child has formed a sound, supportive relationship then they are more likely to express themselves fully and so develop more effective self-regulation mechanisms (Lester and Russell 2008: 71). 'Development is an on-going process, and close, emotionally involving relationships are influential throughout the lifespan. The importance of child-hood may be that the brain structures which mediate social and emotional functioning begin to develop during this time in a manner that appears to be dependent upon interpersonal experience' (Siegel 2001, cited in Lester and Russell 2008: 71). Children can make these relationships only with people and places where they feel safe; adults may be a part of that environment but cannot teach children these things – they need to do it for themselves.

While much more could be said on this wide-ranging issue (and interested readers should look to the section on resilience in Lester and Russell's litera-ture review, 2008), for now it is enough to note that play has a vital role in developing the links and attachments that help shape resilience and the ability to deal with and survive life's many challenges. If children are denied or prevented from these experiences and opportunities they may not thrive as well as they could; this lack of opportunity is called play deprivation.

No play: the effects of play deprivation

If we recognize that play is good for making connections in a child's brain, good for muscular growth and coordination, for socialization, making friends and cognitive development and creativity, then not playing or being deprived of play opportunities would have a detrimental effect on the child. The effects of play deprivation are complex as there are many factors that affect the growing child and there are always exceptions to the rule, children who will play and thrive in extreme conditions; however, the three main causes of play deprivation are the child, the environment and others (usually adults).

It may seem strange that children limit their own play, but looking at the characteristics of play, being in a sufficiently safe place, both physically and psychologically, is a necessary factor. Children under stress will do what they can to survive before they begin to play; if the stress factors continue long enough, the child experiences severe play deprivation. Most self-imposed play deprivation will come from feelings of fear or insecurity prompted by others or by the environment, whether those feelings are real or imagined. Though rare there are instances in the modern world of carers who lock up their children, isolating them from contact with others and play spaces; the child's response on being freed is to seek nourishment and other basic needs for survival rather than play. Work with animals has shown that if the play deprivation is short-lived, the animals bounce back and play more, almost as if they were trying to catch up; however if the deprivation goes on too long, then the brain structures and systems will be affected (Vieira *et al.* 2005; Cui *et al.* 2006).

The effects of adults' actions on children may be seen in the extended play deprivation experienced by a large group of Romanian orphans, which came to the attention of a wider community after the fall of the Communist government in 1989. As a result of government policies, the number of orphans rose during the regime, while the support to orphanages fell as a result of economic savings. In 1989 it was discovered that some children had been tied to their cots for the majority of their early childhood, unable to interact with others, and were treated as subhuman by some of their carers. Some of the children were adopted by families from the USA and UK and were the subject of later research. When Beckett *et al.* (2006) reported on the progress of the Romanian adoptees (compared to English adoptees) they found that the early effects of institutionalized care had lasting effects on the cognitive ability of the children, though there was good improvement shown by some of the most affected. This finding was consistent with the outcomes of the Therapeutic Playwork project (Webb and Brown 2003), which did intervention playwork with orphans in Romania and found that some of the children who were limited in size (compared to active peers) and considered by their carers to be brain damaged were able to respond positively when offered a stimulus and appropriate play cues (Sturrock and Else 1998).

The effects of play deprivation caused by the environment have already been touched on, though it follows that if an environment is impoverished (i.e. lacking balanced stimulation opportunities) then children will not be able to play to the extent of their abilities and desires. Additionally the longer this environmental deprivation goes on, the more 'normal' it may be considered by the adults and children who use that environment. Some key elements for a stimulating space have been mapped on to the Integral Play Framework (Table 4.4 – *Elements for play provision*), yet the simple fact is that children need to be able to exercise their bodies, minds and emotions, exploring varied environments that give them access to others in those environments. While it is true that children will play in the spaces they are in, the more stimulating those spaces are, the more they will be able to play.

As animals we evolved to live in an econiche to which an individual must adapt; Hughes (2012) reminds us that the niche that *Homo sapiens* evolved to fill was the Middle Stone Age world between 40,000 and 15,000 years ago – the Environment of Evolutionary Adaptedness, as Bowlby called it. That environment would have had many challenges to overcome – wild animals, poisonous snakes, insects and plants, fast and deep water, high places such as cliffs and trees, and warring communities, armed only with stone axes and spears. Hughes summed up his concerns about how modern children are deprived by not having access to a similar world: 'The modern environment offers little opportunity for evolutionary play, and ... contains numerous different psychological and physical ingredients to which we are not adapted as a species and that are harmful' (Hughes 2012: 214). While humans as a species should be concerned about our disconnection from the planet, we cannot return to the Stone Age and the challenges it gave us for locomotor play and social play, among other types – we have moved on to more cognitive and intellectual forms of play, which are increasingly being satisfied through computer-based technology.

In recognizing the effects of play deprivation, adults should do all that is possible to help children access a variety of environments, including natural and unpredictable elements, in which they feel safe, psychologically and physically, and of which adults should understand the value and benefit so that they encourage more play and experimentation. In the twenty-first century, too many children are being denied stimulating places to play because of the changes in the environment away from bio-diverse landscapes into concrete jungles, and because too many adults believe that such 'modern' environments are preferable to less comfortable ones without access to constant heat, hot water and every modern gadget. The impact of technology has affected humans for the past 200 years but has escalated dramatically in the last 30 with the increase in available energy and computer-based technology; how this is affecting children's play will be discussed next.

Technology: some of the risks

In looking at the everydayness of play, it is necessary to look at the most recent phenomena of play, playing though some form of electronic device. In just 40 years, electronic games have gone from simple ping-pong games, arcade games like Asteroids™, Space Invaders™ and Pacman™ to home-based systems with all of these and much more as the technology multiplied and the cost of computing came down. In less than a generation, games have moved from copies of arcade games into areas not considered before: the action-adventure game, 'beat 'em up' games, computer role-playing video games, fighting games, 'hack and slash', platform games, racing games, rhythm games and survival horror games, to name just a few. Many of these are now available directly online so that players may interact with gamers on the other side of the world, with the most recent developments into multi-tasking tools such as mobile phones and hand-held systems.

The UK communications regulator Ofcom (2011) stated that 91 per cent of children lived in a UK household with internet access through a PC or laptop. Some 65 per cent of 5–7 year olds made use of a PC or laptop at home to get online, and the figures rise as children grow older – 85 per cent of 8–11s, and 93 per cent of 12–15s.

In 2012 it updated its figures, saying that children are texting and spending even more time online (Ofcom 2012). Texting had become more prolific among 12–15 year olds, who said they were sending an average of 193 texts every week. That had more than doubled from 2011, when just 91 were sent; and was almost four times as many as the UK average of 50 texts per week. The new report also revealed the increasing role of the internet in children's lives. For the first time, 12–15 year olds were spending as much time on the internet as they did watching TV – an estimated 17 hours a week on each activity. For the first time research was carried out on 3–4 year olds and it was discovered that almost one in ten (9 per cent) used a tablet at home, according to their parents. The research also suggested that this age group spent an estimated 15.5 hours watching TV every week and one-third (33 per cent) had a TV in their bedroom.

Researchers for the UK Medical Research Council looked at a representative sample of more than 11,000 children born between 2000 and 2002 (Parkes *et al.* 2013). Almost two-thirds (65 per cent) of the 5 year olds included in the study watched TV for between one and three hours a day, 15 per cent watched more than three hours, with less than 2 per cent watching no television at all. Those who watched television for longer than three hours per day (15 per cent) were more likely after their seventh birthday to develop anti-social behaviours such as fighting, stealing or bullying, according to their mothers' reports. The Medical Research Council team who studied the primary school pupils said it was wrong to link bad behaviour directly to TV viewing, saying other influences, such as parenting styles and social standards, also probably explained the link.

Researchers also say that it is too soon to assume a causal link between TV, technology and children's behaviour patterns, and that too many other factors could have a bearing on the effects, such as children and parents' motivations, access to resources both physically and economically, cultural and social standards (Parkes *et al.* 2013). Yet many people are commenting on the rise in overweight children in the west (and also in developing countries) and noticing that 17 hours a week each on TV and computers does not leave a lot of waking time for other activities. And while some researchers highlight that many online activities are social in nature, others emphasize the growth of cyber-bullying.

The UK government was concerned about this in 2007 and asked Professor Tanya Byron to carry out an investigation into computer technology and the dangers to children of various activities; she reported her findings in the report *Safer Children in a Digital World* (2008). While the incidences of use have changed since the report came out, the main themes are still relevant.

Byron commented on the apparent link between inactivity and the rise in the numbers of children being overweight. Since 2008 the figures have shown an increase, and according to the Royal College of Paediatrics and Child Health, 'half of all UK seven-year-olds are sedentary for six to seven hours every day and are failing to undertake the recommended daily minimum level of physical activity' (Campbell 2013). The report also commented that, at 7, an age at which children should be moving around a lot and enjoying active play, they were 'glued to screens' (Campbell 2013).

Byron (2008), reporting on the effects of technology, also spoke about the isolation experienced by some children when using their computers and screen. Rather than mingling with others of their own age, children were exposed to the whole World Wide Web and its many influences, both educational and predatory. Byron commented that the isolation made some children more subject to cyber-bullying as it was easier for the bully to reach victims; others were less likely to notice it and take action to support the victim. Similarly, for a generation raised protected from stranger-danger and life in the streets, technology was considered to have contributed to a lack of confidence and reduced social skills in some young people using the internet; this led to the young people being open to exploitation and a series of small but high-profile cases in the media (BBC 2013), some of which resulted tragically in suicide by the victim after being harassed by bullies for the actions and images they had been recorded viewing.

'Sexting' – the practice of sending explicit content or images to mobile phone users – was considered a high-risk activity by Byron. Because of the almost universal use of mobile and smart phones by young people, they had come to be seen as intimate means of communication between users. However, as Byron later commented, for an underage girl to send an explicit photo to her boyfriend was not an offence, if he then sent that to a friend or wider afield, not only was he breaching her trust but he was committing a crime under the current UK law. As Byron got into the habit of saying when commenting in these matters, 'If you would not put it on a T-shirt and wear it around town, don't put it on the internet'. Only a few years ago such playful activities would be confined to local woodland or 'behind the bike shed'; now it is possible for images to fly around the planet within hours of being shared.

The good news about predation of children on the internet was that Byron (2008) found little evidence of grooming, where adults pose as young people to meet and abuse them; she considered grooming a low risk, though of course significant for those children and young people affected.

In contrast to the Byron report (2008), children in the UK have high levels of confidence online, with 83 per cent of 8–11 year olds and 93 per cent of 12–15s saying that they were confident that they knew how to stay safe online (Ofcom 2012). As the evidence of bullying, exploitation and sexting may indicate otherwise, some agencies have been set up to help children and young people understand the threat posed by using the internet. The Child Exploitation and Online Protection (CEOP) Centre, supported by the UK Police Authority has also benefited from the advice of Professor Byron. Offering advice for children, parents and guardians, CEOP has a variety of interactive sites for children from 5 years to adulthood. These sites were designed to help children use the internet with an awareness of the risks. Though Byron made clear that she considers the responsibility for internet safety the same as for road safety, or understanding the risks of fires and electricity in the home, it is the responsibility of parents to set up systems that help children use the internet sensibly. Just as many parents would not leave pornographic magazines or DVDs around the home, neither should they leave access to such images online. Content may be controlled by the use of software programs or by the use of the 'off' switch after a few hours' use.

These examples show how the everydayness of play has changed in just a few years; while risks may have been more physical and environmental for previous generations, they are now virtual and closer to home.

A final comment on technology

Some writers speak in support of technology and consider it one of the ways to help humankind survive the next 100 years. Consider Jane McGonigal (2011), who said that gamers globally spend '3 billion hours a week' online and that *World of Warcraft*™ takes the average player 'a total of five hundred hours of gameplay to develop his or her avatar to the game's current maximum level, which is where many players say the fun *really* starts' (emphasis in the original, 2011: 54). McGonigal makes a good argument for why so many people seek excitement and happiness through a gamepad, that the activities are satisfying, there is the hope of being successful, social connection with others with similar interests, giving lives meaning, being part of 'something larger than ourselves' (2011: 49). Clearly computers tap in to something basic within the human psyche, though overall the emphasis on the virtual world can seem hollow and disconnected from reality. Citing Thompson, McGonigal recognizes that some players have *gamer regret*; that 'somewhere around twenty hours a week [most gamers] start to wonder if they're perhaps missing out on real life' (McGonigal 2011: 43). Despite these concerns, McGonigal (2011: 13) argues that, 'Games, in the twenty-first century, will be a primary platform for enabling the future'. Games, she states, will increase career satisfaction, fix our educational systems, treat depression, obesity, anxiety and attention deficit disorder, and 'tackle global-scale problems like climate change and poverty'. Following the Integral Play Framework, a more likely scenario is that, with a balance of activities, both physical and cerebral, social and cultural, humans are more likely to survive the next 50 years with their hands on soil and in the water as well as occasionally on a keyboard.

Playing a computer game is not ultimately creative; the players are playing in someone else's imagination, as has been said by others (Eno 1996: 401). And, compared to the richness of traditional stories or well-written tales, computer games, with some exceptions, are often weak in morality, mythology and imagination. If one of the aims is for children to learn the rules about life, society and how to get on with people, it is better to do that in the real world, where shooting someone with a laser gun has consequences, and rebooting is not possible when your guinea pig dies.

We cannot 'un-invent' computers, they are akin to bows and arrows in a previous age – and there are too many homes where well-meaning parents banned TV and/or computers for their young children only to find they became 'addicted' to the electronic experience when finally exposed to it, as they would be through school, clubs or friendship groups. Children will always find ways to play with what they are interested in. Young people attending a church group at the behest of their parents were asked to make a video for Sunday school; they used the digital camera to make a pornographic movie instead (Neil 2013). If children do not experience things in their life there is very little chance of them appreciating it; play indoors a bit, play outdoors a bit, play passively a bit, play actively a bit. Parents who want to play with their children need to invest a little time to meet the children halfway – for example, by having family days where everyone in the family takes it in turns to decide what to do. That way, the 9 year old wanting to go ten-pin bowling gets their wish and the parent wanting to go cycling gets what they want. Perhaps both adults and children are likely to say, 'Oh no' to start with, but then find out that the different activities were more fun than was originally thought.

Everyday play is what children get up to in their own lives, in their own way. There is no agenda to what they do; they do it as it is engaging and satisfying, usually if it has been self-chosen. The opportunities to play in the twenty-first century are quite varied compared to earlier generations but carry the same interest for children; finding out about each other, exploring the world and beginning to make a difference in it. In addition to playing at home and in the street, children may play everywhere in the real and virtual worlds; they will be healthier if they have the chance to balance these activities in their daily lives.

Questions to help practitioners understand everydayness and the darker side of play

- How often do you see children saying 'No'? What issues does this cause for them, for you? What rules do you have for children? Are those the same as rules you apply to adults; if not, why not? What would be the minimum number of rules that you could use?
- What forms of deep play are you aware of? Is deep play something encouraged by you? Is deep play always a physical form of play; do you

consider that sexting might be a form of deep play? Do you think it practical to support deep play? If not, what do you consider the effects of play deprivation to be?

- Do you consider that play is part of everyday life? If so, should adults ever intervene? If play will happen anyway, what is the adult's role? How could society recognize the everyday value of play for children; what would the five key actions be?

7
Developing reflective practice and creative approaches

Making sense of play and supporting children in their play are complex issues. As we have seen, play can happen everywhere yet by thinking carefully about play, children and play spaces, adults may improve the opportunities for play immensely. Some people observing play believe it to be a simple activity that needs no adult support or intervention, yet the signs of dysplay are all around, and those who have supported children though the profession of playwork know that careful, considerate and creative approaches to work with children can work wonders. When working with children in their play it is important to be curious and skilled in sensitive assessments of the children's play cues, to understand the value and benefits of play and that engagement in play is the child's choice and cannot be forced or prolonged. It is also important to reflect often on both the activities of the day and our response to them. The Integral Play Framework provides a useful model against which to assess practice. What is the 'best' approach to take when reflecting on our work? What gets in the way? What tools can be used?

Reflection in this sense implies considering actions undertaken, thinking about what happened, contemplating the effects of various actions, and musing about the future; what could happen next. Some writers do not consider the term *reflection* very helpful (Bolton 2010), for a reflection on something bad is still something bad, but as with any human endeavour, do we accept the first presentation or do we inquire beneath the skin? Not going through a full reflective cycle means that we are only seeing part of the picture and if we don't have time to do the job right first time, when will we have time to do it again? Full reflection requires us to examine the obvious and then go a little further.

Single-loop and double-loop learning

There have been many theorists on the practice of reflection though two of the most influential have been Argyris and Schön (1978) who wrote about single-loop and double-loop learning. When people reflect on what has happened in a situation, they often tend to look at the expected outcome and work with the variables they can control to effect a conclusion – this Argyris and Schön called *single-loop learning*. However, when people look at the surrounding conditions and begin to question them, wishing to make changes, this becomes *double-loop learning* – practice may change yet also the conditions in which the practice occurs. So to bring it back to supporting play, single-loop learning may help make a particular activity better; double-loop learning would help look at the activity in context and how it fits within the child's world and the setting it was being delivered through. For example, the need for outdoor play with children may be recognized in wider society and provision made for children's playgrounds. However, by thinking more widely, it can be seen that helping children access the whole environment offers better opportunities all round, and the need for specific provision becomes redundant. The key to making the best of a service is to reflect deeply and consistently.

Cyclical models

Following Argyris and Schön there have been several cyclical models that emphasize different parts of the reflective process. Kolb (1984) stressed learning from experience so that the new awareness may be applied to practice, relying heavily on cognitive thinking, as explained by Piaget (1962). Having had a concrete experience, an experience in the world, the practitioner would apply reflective observation to that experience, perhaps making notes but certainly reflecting consciously on the experiences, possibly with feedback from others. Using those reflections the learner would then think about the concepts underpinning that experience; what was the purpose of the activity, did it do what was intended and, if so, how? Using the concepts identified the practitioner would then try a new action in the world to see how the experience may be changed, thinking about the activity in terms of logical theory that is understood by the reflector, so that 'ownership' of the activity preferably develops. The ideal use of this model would be in a cyclical way, adding to the knowledge gained first time around the loop, though of course some practitioners may be reliving the same experience time and time again, consciously or not, so that after five years' work, all they have is one year's experience repeated five times.

Gibbs (1988) added to Kolb's work with a shared debriefing, carried out with another practitioner/learner, allowing the possibility for a deeper and wider reflection. Following an event, the practitioner would be asked to describe what happened in as objective a way as possible. The second stage was to examine the learner's feelings and reactions to the situation, again objectively if they were able. Next came evaluation, asking what was good or bad about the experience from the practitioner's point of view; this would necessarily be subjective. The fourth stage would look at the analysis of the situation; using existing theory and concepts, could the reflector make sense of the situation? Would other people have acted the same way – if so why, if not then why not? From this analysis a conclusion would be made of the lessons to be learned both for the practitioner and in general, looking at the personal and wider implications of the situation – adding some *double-loop learning*. The final action would be to put the thinking/learning into practice, identifying the things that would be different next time and the steps to be taken to make changes in practice.

Writing within a nursing environment, Johns' model of reflection (2000) again required a focused effort by the practitioners to share their views with another through a series of structured questions, describing the experience then examining the causes of the event, the essential factors that contributed to it. Looking at the context was valuable to add depth through trying to understand the significant background factors to the experience. Following this clarifying process, the reflection would start with a series of questions looking at the actions of the practitioners and others first, then at the feelings of the reflector and then others' feelings about the experience when it was happening. With recognition of double-loop learning (Argyris and Schön 1978), the questions then focused on influencing factors, internal factors and external factors that may have affected decision making. The final stages of the process included evaluation of the responses and whether different actions may have resulted in a better outcome, before applying any learning through asking whether the experience changed ways of knowing and working. Johns' approach, while valuable in reflecting on an incident requiring deep analysis and with the benefit of time, was not practical for busy people working on a daily basis with children.

Reflecting on practice, in practice and before practice

Adding to his own work, Schön recognized the difficulty of double-loop reflection when he described the practice of *reflexivity* (reflecting on the reflection, taking nothing for granted – examining first principles) as a *swamp* (Bolton 2010). The metaphor adds to our understanding of reflection by suggesting that the real world of people and children is messy, as a swamp is – there is no clear way through, the way needs to be uncovered by exploration and investigation. The swamp is no place for rules, laws and schedules, or for mechanical, efficient systems – it is the opposite of the rational predictable approach to life and action that planning may suggest. When working with people, and especially with children, the need for flexibility, creativity and quick thinking is important. Reflecting on past experience is valuable, but so is reflecting on what is happening in the moment.

Again we should be reminded that, when playing, children do not need adults to be present, though when they are, they should do their best not to make the experience worse for the child; being consciously present in the space should help with that outcome.

Others have added to Schön's ideas with the concept of *mindfulness* (Kabat-Zinn 1991) or *reflection-before-action*. Mindfulness, borrowing from a Buddhist principle, is the focusing of attention and awareness, paying attention on purpose, in the present moment and, as far is possible, non-judgementally (it has been referred to earlier as the *witness position*). Darwin (2010) uses the idea to differentiate between what he calls *beginner* and *expert mind*.

When starting a new practice or way of operating, beginners often have many possibilities open to them, the route through the undergrowth (or indeed swamp) had not been trodden before; any way is as good as any other. Beginners have not yet learned how to behave, so possibilities are many, though the beginner may have fears of failure, of doing the task 'wrong'. By contrast, experts have found 'the right route', they know what to do and where to go; if they are complacent they will focus on getting the job done 'right' – they will know the most efficient way to work. However, in many situations in the modern world – and especially when working with children – doing *the right thing* may mean being flexible and responsive rather than having a set response. This is where Darwin brings in the concept of *mindfulness*; by being mindful, the adult is able to *reflect-before-action* and is able to retain some of the qualities of a beginner in their skill set. Mindfulness helps us avoid falling into the mode of 'automatic pilot' or mindlessness (Weick and Sutcliffe 2007); a mindless mental style works to conceal problems that may be worsening, it is a tendency towards a style of mental functioning in which people follow recipes, impose old categories with some rigidity to classify what they experience, and mislabel unfamiliar new contexts as familiar old ones. It is a way of making sense of the world that owes nothing to how the world is now but how it was seen by the adult/expert in the past. Darwin (2010) suggests that, before acting on instinct or auto-pilot, we strive to remain mindful and so aware of what is happening, our emotions and our actions in response to what we see. By being mindful we are able to see the situation, our response to that situation and therefore what actions we might take to help.

A useful tool for helping remember the three parts of this approach is that proposed by Rolfe *et al.* (2001), who ask three simple questions: What,

So What and Now What? The questions help practitioners reflect and respond to the various issues of an event – what is happening now; what are the effects of that event and what should be done as a result of that reflection? The three questions may be responded to superficially, or over an extended period and with lots of consideration; as always, the process of reflection is controlled by the reflector, and is led or limited by their own knowledge and experience.

Levels and depth in reflection: the U Model

A student of Argyris developed a new theory about change and learning in 2005 which showed different ways that individuals may respond to a situation. Peter Senge and colleagues (2005) conceived the 'U Model' to show how practice may be implemented on a number of levels. The concept is named the U Model, or U Theory, as it asks reflectors to take an experience, reflect on it a little and then propose some action; as the reflection becomes deeper, the 'U' becomes more pronounced, going through levels that ask for cognitive, emotive and conscious responses. Arising from their work with organizations, the group found that people in organizations were being confronted with complex, intractable problems that often had the following characteristics: (1) the solutions to identified problems were not known; (2) the problems being dealt with were going to evolve over time and were only partially known at the start; and (3) the key actors needed in order to be successful were not fully known (Hall 2007). The model was a move away from more mechanistic models that required participants to go through a series of steps; the aim was to create a way of responding in the moment to the experience, to be fully present in the experience.

> Leaders need a different kind of capacity that helps them deal with situations that are emerging. The traditional decision-making model, which assumes that you have all the knowledge about the alternatives and preferences, is no longer useful or valid . . .
> You may have a whole repertoire of stylized behaviours, but you have honed an awareness that prepares you for the most stressful, demanding, and uncertain situations. When acting under stress in real life situations, you are not going to have time to go back and read a bunch of books, and even if you did, it wouldn't help you.
> *Peter Senge and Otto Scharmer (in Hall 2007: 7–9)*

The model has a number of levels, which were called reacting, redesigning and reframing before arriving at *presencing* (or mindfulness, as was described earlier). Table 7.1 shows the levels, and links them to the work of others who have considered similar matters.

The first level is called *downloading*, where the practitioner accepts information in a passive or neutral fashion. The person then takes that information and reacts to it using accepted means of practice; the information leads to *institutionalizing*. An example would be a practitioner who understands a play concept such as a play cue or a play type, processing the information seen, they are able to act in a formal way to what they have experienced – 'I can recognize and label the play cues that children can offer'. While a skill in itself, this act adds little to the original experience.

Next comes *seeing objectively*, or *seeing with new eyes*, where the practitioner processes information in an objective manner. The person then takes that information and *redesigns* it using new ways of practice; the information leads to *prototyping* or developing new actions based on the information gathered. An example would be a practitioner who understands that play takes place in environments that offer play opportunities, processing the information they have, they are able to change their reactions based on what they have seen – 'I can support children's play by creating environments or talking to others about how we work'. This level adds a sense of change to the experience, allowing for interaction with what is expressed through the child's actions. In later explanations of the theory Senge describes this as the *open mind* level.

The third part of the model was *sensing holistically*, and practitioners engage their senses and heart in the work. By collecting information in a holistic manner, they are able to consider cognitive and emotional issues, using such tenuous approaches as intuiting – what feels right. This approach then leads to *reframing* of the issue in a new light and multiple options for action become apparent. As Senge and team put it, *crystallizing from options* – making new actions from the situation to see what results they produce. In this position, 'There is no decision making. What needs to be done will just emerge from the process' (Scharmer, in Hall 2007: 7). Of course this is a paradox, for the results do not just appear, but emerge from the deep reflection and awareness applied to the situation by the person doing the reflection, though with an awareness of the pressures involved in the situation. An example for an adult supporting play would be that they recognize that they are willing to change themselves or the environment to create more stimuli and more opportunity for new forms of play.

The descriptions of the model explained so far rely on past actions to collect information and project it into a future not yet realized, the two sides of the U. However, the turning point of the U is considered by Senge to be 'Now' – if we are fully aware in the moment, we are *present*, neither in the past nor the future, and aware of what is happening; we are mindful. In this state we are aware of what is happening around us, of ourselves and of our actions in the world; some might say we are consciously alive. By remaining mindful during an activity, we are able to *reflect-in-action*; we may witness the

Table 7.1 Reflection and its roles in practice.

U Model (Senge et al. 2005)	Approach to learning (Ramsden 1988)	Type of reflection (Moon 2006)	Action	Example
		Noticing	Perceiving, superficial observation	I see children playing
Reacting – institutionalizing; labelling actions	**'Surface'**	**Making sense**	Connections are made to existing forms of understanding	I can recognize play cues that children issue
		Making meaning	Understanding indicates the underlying purposes or significance	The types of play cue suggest children have different interests and skills
Redesigning – prototyping; trying new things to see what works		**Working with meaning**	Reflection is presented meaningfully; spoken or in writing, in presentation, in action, etc.	I can support that play by creating environments or talking to others about how we work
Reframing – crystallizing actions from emergent options	**'Deep'**	**Transformative practice**	Willingness to change thoughts and mind-set, full evaluation	I'm willing to change myself or the environment to create more stimulus and more opportunity for new forms of play
The turning point of the U Presencing – Now (mindfulness)			Questioning of self and project Looking for meaning	Why are we here? Do I need to change; does anything else need changing?

activity, and decide what to do there and then, confident that our actions will be informed by our choices and awareness.

Other models

Others have commented on similar phenomena; Ramsden (1988) spoke about 'surface' and 'deep' learning, where surface learning was uncritically accepting new facts and ideas, learning how to apply ideas without understanding background factors, whereas deep learning involved looking for meaning, analytically examining facts and ideas, before linking them into existing cognitive structures and making links between ideas. Moon (2006) produced a range of actions from noticing, through making sense, making meaning and working with meaning, then transformative practice. These ideas are compared in the Table 7.1 – *Reflection and its roles in practice*.

This approach indicates that knowledge, awareness and methods of response increase the deeper into the model we go. This process needs to be conscious and chosen; simply understanding the model is not enough to make people aware and mindful or present. Reflection requires that we engage on a journey of discovery with an openness and willingness to learn; without that we will inevitably become comfortable and perhaps 'stick' at one level or another. The cliché of continuous improvement holds good here; we need to be willing to continually improve the project that is ourselves – our skills, knowledge and ability – and then we will begin to experience and understand the insights that the different approach brings.

Making reflection a good habit

The process of refection is better when it becomes automatic; with practice it becomes a habit and not a chore. It should not be carried out mechanically but with an awareness of what is trying to be achieved by the action and then the conscious reflection.

Start before action

Why is the task necessary? **How** could it be carried out? **What** specific tasks are needed? Starting with *Why* helps identify the value base for the work, which will help set motivation and interest when the task becomes more challenging, when the going gets tough. Asking why will help tap in to the base drives and instincts that support and motivate us. People avoid asking *Why* as it is often the 'big question' – it is easier to come up with to-do lists and rationalize what is needed and how this can be applied, but the basic reason for something is frequently overlooked. As examples, are you in the business of providing play opportunities for children (*What*), are you working outdoors to access nature (*How*), or are you wanting to help children have an engaged and satisfying childhood, where they make as many choices as possible (*Why*)? Starting with the *Why* gives many more options for action (indoors/ outdoors; organized provision/informal provision; home/neighbourhood/; regular/one off, etc.). Starting with *What* may limit actions to only those tasks that you have identified, or may take more energy to change direction if that is needed.

It may help to answer the following questions:

- Why did you choose to work with children?
- What motivates you to work with children?
- What needs in you are fulfilled by this choice?

Being aware of what drives you helps when things get rough or challenging as they will from time to time. If you feel you are 'just doing a job' it is easier to stop when it gets hard; if you feel you are working towards one of your life goals or to improve the quality of life for someone else, you will find the energy to dig a little deeper.

During action

As far as is possible, be aware of your actions in the space – how are you using your body, what are you feeling, what are you thinking, how are you getting on with/relating to others in the space, what roles are you taking or are others taking? Try to be objective about your interactions with others; though not wholly divorced from the action, you should still be apart from what is happening in the children's play. As circumstances allow, try to be playful without playing; the play belongs to the children, and you do not want to adulterate or contaminate that, but being playful helps your affect, the way you relate to others and how they see you. A playful face is a much better starting place than a stern or authoritarian appearance.

The Integral Play Framework can be a useful tool for reflection during action (as well as before and after action). Being aware of our subjective feelings and thoughts helps us think about the psychological and cultural aspects of our behaviour and relationships with others. Remembering the objective, factual elements means we can focus on the physical – our bodies and the spaces we occupy – but also the social, the roles and responsibilities we and others have in the space.

Our responses can only be within the abilities we hold at any time as explained above, however by thinking of these four domains, and applying them to the frame of the playing child we are able to think about ways of supporting play opportunities; by applying them to the frame of ourselves with playing children, we are able to think of our influence in the play space; and by applying them to the frame of the space within a wider culture we can identify the elements that need support or challenge; operating in this holistic mode would be presencing (Senge *et al.* 2005), and mindful (Darwin 2010).

After an event

Using a tool or approach of your choice, think about what has happened; what was expected? Did the event go as you expected – if so, how; if not, why not? Some practitioners reflect directly after work in a diary or learning journal, others set aside time for reflection once a day, once a week and sometimes once a year. (For an annual review, to look back at what has changed over that period, are you the person you thought you were at the start of the year? See below for more guidance.)

When reflecting in a tool like a learning journal, it may be useful to have a consistent format to help explore patterns in the work. The following may be a useful starting point:

When: day/date – time of year/weather

Where: location – where you were, what kind of space it was

Who: children present – their ages, genders, other background details

Who: teamwork – what other adults were present, who was doing what?

What: factors affecting children's play – locally, and in the wider environment

Why: theory – what links can you make from what was experienced to what writers say about play?

What next: practice development – what changes would you like to make, and why?

Any other issues? Other ideas?

Whatever format is used, the act of reflection itself is useful, and it helps with bringing awareness into the moment to reflect as honestly as you can on what happened. The act of recording and reviewing is important, as it builds up useful data for later processing.

Journals may be used for a number of other uses, the first of which is the weekly reflection, where it is possible to identify the things that emerged that could be developed for the following week. When planning for short-term goals it may be helpful to set yourself at least one task, though no more than four, for fear of being distracted or swamped by the planning actions and not having time for the interaction with or support of children.

Evaluations and appraisals

A journal/personal diary may also be used for recording meetings with others; staff, other professionals, parents and partners. By carrying it around constantly, a journal may be useful on long journeys for more reflection, planning new projects, making notes, compiling to-do lists, composing poems . . . The point is that the journal becomes a focus for thinking 'off the job'; it becomes a means for logging thoughts and for seeing connections between activities and ideas. It then happens to be useful for evaluations both formal (work related) and informal (interest related), and as a prompt for future planning.

When used for professional purposes, the evaluation can focus on work standards, setting policies, goals and targets, checking that these are 'fit for purpose' as necessary. When thinking about your own interests, the refection may be more personal, examining feelings, your own theories about what you do and why you do it, working at your 'own level' – whatever you take that to be.

The Integral Play Framework can also be used to help frame your responses and thoughts for evaluations and appraisals, whether professional and work related or informal. The Framework helps with making reflection holistic, by exploring feelings and actions, as they affect us and others. The four quadrants are useful prompts to help focus thinking.

For example, looking at **professional evaluations** using the upper-left quadrant, we can explore confidence and identity, and check if we are providing sensory experiences, opportunities for adults to listen to children and develop empathy for their points of view. Does our work encourage problem solving, and provide opportunities and support for risk and challenge? If not what can we do about it? The upper-right quadrant focuses on physical development, providing opportunities to access the four elements, providing height, depth, width, movement and textures, 'loose parts', costumes, props, supporting easy and continual contact with these features, and encouraging change (and destruction) in the environment. The lower-left quadrant is about cultural understanding, providing art, craft and music-making opportunities, places to tell stories, sing songs, supporting quiet (and noisy) spaces, and making available experiences from different cultures, to help celebrate different festivals. And the lower-right quadrant looks at social issues, starting with being a friend to someone else, then chatting/debating, leading, joining in and following activities, explaining about rights (and responsibilities), and raising ecological and political issues when appropriate.

Using the Framework for **personal reflection** and development can work on a number of levels. Following Moon's process (2006) we can go through noticing experiences, making sense of them, to making meaning, working with meaning and then transformative practice. These questions are not to-do lists; they are intended as prompts for you to engage with as you choose.

Confidence and identity (upper-left quadrant)

- Do you notice and explore your perceptions and feelings, the sensations in your body?
- What does your 'sixth sense', your intuition, tell you about yourself and your work?
- What stories and symbols emerge in the work, what aspects are fantastical (out of this world) or archetypal?
- How often do you feel enjoyment in your work, what modes of creativity do you use regularly?
- When and where are you able to express satisfaction?
- Are you 'problem seeking' or problem solving?
- Why are you doing what you do; how do you rationalize your thoughts and feelings?

Physical development (upper-right quadrant)

- How often do you explore your world using smell, touch, taste, sight, sound – as well as other senses such as awareness of your body, movement in space?
- Do you experience running, jumping, testing your strength, movement and speed?
- What practice do you have that enhances coordination and movements and actions, exploring balance and delicate actions?
- When and where are you able to make changes in the world, adapting and designing spaces in the environment?
- When do you experiment, developing prototypes, displaying your mastery of physical media?

Cultural understanding (lower-left quadrant)

- What activities do you choose to do, prefer to do by yourself?
- When and where do you prefer to follow others or work on your own?
- How often do you cooperate, working on projects that involve imagination, drama, music?
- In what circumstances do you conform to what is expected, when do you dig your heels in and rebel, or assert views as your own?

- What beliefs do you live by? Who do you respect, really? Which values do you accept, and which do you challenge?
- How often do you celebrate initiations (new beginnings), special events and rituals throughout the day, the week, the year?
- How do you wind down at the end of the day or when feeling stressed? Who do you talk to?

Social issues (lower-right quadrant)

- What roles or work tasks do you do best operating alone?
- Who are your best friends? The people you can talk to about anything, communicating in confidence?
- What groups do you get on well with – families, friends, workmates, extended family? Anyone?
- Are you comfortable doing team activities with friends and/or strangers?
- Can you take any role in a task or project, or do you have preferred functions you do?
- Are you competitive in your roles with others, are you at ease leading activities and caring for others?

Annual review

If you set yourself time aside to do an annual review (or you do one as part of your professional development), it can help to be consistent with the approach and content of your review. Setting-based reviews will often have their own format, though using the questions as above may help you prepare and bring your interests into the process.

Another way of gaining views about your practice and approaches is to enter into dialogue with others, sometimes called 'story making' – creating the story of your experience. Given that contexts and personal opinions are infinitely variable, we can never know the reality of our experience – by the time it has been assessed it has already changed – although the more information we can collect, the better informed we will be. For example, '360° feedback' is a useful system of feedback that has been used in professional circles for a while now and there are companies dedicated to the process, using their own approaches. However, at its simplest, 360° feedback means asking people all around you to comment on your skills, abilities and attitudes as they experience them. It can seem a daunting prospect, yet in practice most people who take part give helpful and constructive comments. The first 360° circle would include the people directly in your workplace, your manager, your colleagues (co-workers and those who report to you) and your clients, who may be children and parents. The 'second' circle would include those people who know you in different ways through your work; if they are willing to do it, comments from funders and inspectors who have worked closely with you or on a project can be very insightful, as can the views of support staff (administrators, accountants, human resources staff) or other part-time or casual staff who work with you at key times. Quite often we can reveal more of our true selves in unguarded moments or when challenged than in routine work.

Starting this process may seem a lot of 'extra work', yet over time it comes together to form an approach to your experience that is supportive, informative, developmental and rewarding; 'Unless you do something beyond what you have already mastered, you will never grow up' (Osborn, in McLellan 1998: 2). Ideally the process becomes one where the changes are incremental, taking you forward in small steps, onwards and upwards, and not round and round the same treadmill.

Peer-supported review

A sometimes simpler and easier introduction to 360° feedback is peer-supported review, when a practitioner and a colleague agree to look at each other's work and offer feedback on what has been done and how the work was handled. Simple yet complex questions, such as why, how and what, will get the review under way. Using the four quadrants from the Integral Play Framework will help determine the focus of your enquiries with your colleagues; what are they feeling, what are they thinking, how are they getting on with/relating to others in the space, what responsibilities are they taking?

* What are co-workers feeling about their practice?
* What is their confidence in a variety of tasks? When are they 'out of their comfort zone'?
* What theories are they using, how are they thinking about and challenging what they do?
* What levels of flexibility and adaptability do they exhibit in their work?
* How conscious are they of the value judgements they use and express at work?
* When do colleagues state they are able to express choice and make a personal contribution in their work?
* Are they able to work with a variety of children who exhibit different types of confidence and attention behaviour?
* How assured are they engaging in dialogue and debate with other colleagues whether in management or in junior positions?

- How often do they offer and seek out two-way feedback?
- What steps do they take to get to know the team especially inducting new staff?
- How confident are they when faced with new situations or practices?
- Are colleagues clear about their roles and responsibilities, both negotiated and assumed?
- Do they have an ethical base from which to work; does it match with that expected in the workplace?
- Are they aware of the steps for compliance with policy and legislation in the setting?
- What evidence is there of their contribution to equity with others, are all involved, all contributing?
- How do they have a say in quality assurance and evaluation systems?
- What types of activity do they engage in at the setting; do these meet the needs of playing children?
- Are they able to use and apply useful generic skills to support their work, e.g. access to information technology, administration and report preparation?
- How many and what type of technical skills does the staff member have, where do they need help?
- Do they know how to access resources, and how to fully utilize the facility?
- Do they use their own time and energy well with their allocated work plan?
- Do they have successful strategies for working with children of different ages, abilities and group size?

As with continuous reflection and 360° feedback, peer-supported review will be only as good as the willingness of the reflector to examine their own practice and their preparedness to change; often getting a good start to reflection is the vital first step to building confidence.

Learning journeys: understanding how your skill set was formed

If reflection is a new activity and an understanding of a practitioner's learning and development activity to date is needed, there are a number of approaches that may be used to identify the key actions.

These approaches/reflective tools ask that practitioners choose a meta-phorical symbol to represent their life to date, and that they indicate on the symbol the key life choices or events that they feel were significant in their life. The completed image is then shared with another to help the reflector consolidate their thinking with some explanation. Some tools use words, though many suggest that pictures or other symbols are used to indicate key events; by drawing one's life it is often easier to access emotional states than by using words, which may seem more revealing or embarrassing. Using symbols allows the reflector to indicate what is significant to them that they are prepared to share, though they do not need to explain everything. For example, events that were important but they do not wish to talk about may be represented by empty boxes, deaths by gravestones without details, and so on. The partners should understand that these are important but taboo and not to be asked about them unless the reflector discloses freely.

Perhaps the most literal tool is a life- or time-line, a line from birth to the reflector's current age, that moves up or down according to good and less-good times. Images or words may be drawn on the line at relevant points to indicate the reason for the change, dates may be used to indicate age, though again drawings such as primary school or marriage may be enough to suggest relevant times. As with all the tools it is often a revelation to recollect what was happening when significant events took place in one's life; people often realize that their most challenging times produced some of the profoundest changes and lessons in their lives.

Other starting images may be chosen according to the whims of the reflector, and are often as revealing as the later content that is added. Listed below are a few ideas.

- A river image, like the life-line is a chronological image that shows time passing, though the image may be used to show turbulent, rocky or calm times with relative ease. Images may be in the stream or on the river bank.

- A key image is the last of the distinct time-related tools. A key with a large circle at one end then a typical 'up and down' key pattern at the other end. The key pattern may be formed by the life experiences of the reflector's life. Reflectors are then encouraged to summarize the three major strengths or skills identified though the tool, and list these in the key end represented by the large circle.

- The image of a tree is good for showing connections, the root indicating where practitioners came from and the significant root systems that led to the trunk of their big achievements, with branches and then leaves showing significant interests and future directions. The tree metaphor also lends itself well to reflectors using sticky notes as leaves so that themes may be clustered or far apart according to interest and issues.

- Another natural image is that of a flower, where the central circle, as with the key image, may be used to list important interests or strengths. The petals are then drawn in varied sizes according to the significance of the topic represented. A major life event such as raising a family may produce a large petal (or series of smaller but linked ones) representing the family. Problems or difficult issues may be shown with smaller, withered leaves or second petals around the first ring – whether the final image is a daisy or a chrysanthemum, depending on the life story of the person. As with all the tools, the content of the petals is best shown with imagery, though words and numbers may be used.

- Problematic for some people, the idea of a shield is useful for others. For those who do not like the martial connotations of a shield a simple circle may be more suitable. The shield represents what skills and experiences have 'protected' the reflector from the challenges of the world. The shield/circle is typically drawn with four quarters: one for early influences, the second for school life, the third quarter for current issues, and the last for future plans and aspirations, though different themes may be used – family, work, personal interests, education.

- One more image is that of a spider's web, good for showing links between stages of life and links to the spider – the reflector – in the middle. These may be shown on each strand, or clusters of issues can be stuck to the web close to the middle or by the edge if less significant.

Begin now!

Reflection is an activity that does not need to wait for 'the right time', it may be started immediately. Choose an approach, a simple one to start with, and diary time to reflect – 15 minutes a day is a good contract with yourself.

Reflection can be even better if it is made fun. Find a partner to work with who shares your sense of humour; it can be easier to admit mistakes with a friend than with a stranger. Reflect flamboyantly – buy a jazzy journal that catches your attention, use motivational messages to get you started, e.g. 'small contributions add up to great effects' (de Bono 1991: 13).

Whatever you choose to do, try to do it without exceptions, keep going; change is hard at first until it becomes second nature. Research suggests that implementing a change so that it sticks is much more successful when it has been carried out for 84 days (about 12 weeks). And of course review after those three months to see if the process still works for you; if not, try another one. Identify and develop your strengths, learn your own lessons, and either learn new skills or decide what to do and what not to do. The fundamental feature of reflection is self-awareness and motivation; by being authentic with ourselves we are more likely to be honest about our abilities and decide to do something to change – and motivation is vital if we are to keep going.

What do you think?

One of the fastest and simplest ways of getting feedback from a group of children, parents, partners or a staff team is a simple target drawn on a flipchart. It can take 30 seconds to set up but give useful feedback on performance or choices that can really change practice.

The flipchart should be drawn with four circles of increasing size – a typical target shape. Two lines are then to be drawn across the middle of the centre circle, horizontally and then vertically to the edge of the outermost edge, to separate the shape into four quarters. The quarters should then be given the themes that are needed for feedback; for a session with children it might be 'fun, messy, playing with friends, do it again!' Or ask them about their favourite outdoor activities – 'building dens, climbing trees, making mud pies, rolling down a bank'. A session with parents might have themes such as 'enjoyable, practical, involving, informative' – the simpler the themes, the easier to understand, but also they may be misunderstood, so a little explanation can be needed.

The group of respondents are then asked as they leave the session to make a mark on the target indicating their satisfaction with the themes named (using a marker pen, a spot or tick will do). 'Very good/excellent' would be a bull's eye, 10; less good would be shown by the tick's distance from the middle; someone using the edge of the paper would be telling you they were not happy with that theme. Five minutes later the flipchart would be full of ticks or spots, visibly showing the group's choices or satisfaction ratings; this information may then be processed to help with reflection and future planning of events or activities.

Reflection gives us the chance to consider in detail or more depth things that we might not otherwise have considered; it is a chance to step outside ourselves for a time to see how we are behaving. But of course reflection without action is meaningless: as Bolton (2010) reminded us, for things to change or improve, we often need to do activities differently, to change our thinking; working creatively gives us just that opportunity.

Why be creative?

We not only perceive the world, we conceive it. We not only have experiences; we have ideas and thoughts about them . . . We make the world we live in and can remake it. What does this tell us about the nature and process of creativity?

Ken Robinson (2011)

Without creative and playful activities, life would be very impoverished, following genetic messages, much as ants in colonies do. Evolution has equipped humans with a magical structure, the brain, which regulates our somatic functions, helps us relate to other creatures, and helps us explore and attempt to understand the world; it seems a missed opportunity not to take full advantage of its capabilities. There are many reasons to be creative, as the benefits of creativity are important to the individual, group and species (Jesson 2012: 11).

Creativity for many people is their way to be 'free'; in a world with many constraints on resources, time and activities, doing something original and unique is a way of saying 'here I am', a way of showing that they exist. Being creative permits the expression of a personal voice and so develops self-awareness; 'who am I, what do I think, why is this important?' Creativity helps people to be genuine and true with themselves, it helps develop authenticity. By being creative people explore their self-concept but also what other people think of them and their output. This process is risky and takes a little courage to get started, but also when changing or challenging oneself. The exploration and flexibility involved in being creative helps us become better problem solvers, more confident with better strategies for overcoming difficulties and finding emerging solutions. People often find themselves 'in the zone' when being creative, when mind and body merge, and 'doingness' takes over; many people report being happiest when fully engrossed in doing what they love (Csikszentmihalyi 1990). This sense of well-being often spills over into the rest of their lives, so helping people feel calmer and easing stress; indeed many people report doing creative activities as a bit of personal time, specifically to carve out some time for themselves, to be themselves. Creativity is good for us.

Creativity is also good for groups, it helps people connect with other people doing similar activities, sharing interests and sharing values – which are often of a wider, more connected nature than being simply pleasure seeking. Creativity in groups helps us realize that it is more than just about intelligence or academic achievement. There are so many ways to be creative and so many manifestations of creativity it becomes clear than there are multiple intelligences (Gardner 1999), and people may be creative using their minds and bodies in different ways, interacting with one another and the environment, learning unique skills and learning about one another.

Is creativity good for the species? The last 40,000 years of human change have shown that, for a hairless, medium-sized ape with a brain larger than average, we are able to adapt quite well to a variety of environments, predators and situations; we could not have done that without being flexible and creative, exploiting the many talents that we possess in spite of other species being stronger, faster or better protected. It may be that our creativity has led to us overusing the resources of the planet, making mountains out of molehills with our ability to turn mud into building materials that allow us to reach towards the sky. But it is certain that our creativity will help keep us going for a few more millennia yet, finding new technologies that give us more energy, more food and more water, or that help us adapt to the environmental changes all round us; having original ideas that have value is good for the human species.

Creativity is multi-modal, it involves thoughts and actions but also different levels of human perception; 'Creativity is not a single power that people have or do not have, but multidimensional . . . It is an attitude: a willingness to reconsider what we take for granted' (Robinson 2011: 137). To be creative we need to use things, concepts and actions in new ways, and often as humans we ascribe meaning to these actions. The various meanings of creativity involve *words* that tend to be logical symbols once learned, and *images* that are usually metaphorical and symbolic in a different way.

The common blockages to creativity

> Creativity involves breaking out of established patterns in order to look at things in a different way.
>
> *Edward de Bono (1992)*

As Einstein is credited with saying, it is not possible to solve problems with the thinking that created them; repeating actions takes us round and round the same paths – we need to find new directions if we are to have new experiences. However, most people find being creative difficult for many reasons; Robinson (2009: 132) describes the barriers to creativity as personal, social and cultural, three concentric 'circles of constraint', which impact on the individual.

The personal circle of constraint is affected by fear, self-doubt and self-confidence – individuals not believing in their creativity and their ability. Fear is often fear of failure, but people also carry fears of not being good enough, not having the right level of skill, looking foolish and fear of the unknown. The educational paradigm can be responsible for many of these fears; the expectation that we need to get things right and do well (i.e. produce a recognized outcome) and that failure is not acceptable. But, as Robinson points out it, 'If you are not prepared to be wrong you'll never come up with anything original' (2009: 15). Personal constraints can lead to the development of a bad habit with regard to creativity, not to try to be creative so there is no chance of failure – as Erich Fromm stated, 'Creativity requires the courage to let go of certainties'.

The expectations of others often result in feelings of guilt about doing something new, especially if the others are in the immediate social circle. The obligations an individual feels towards others are often considered more important than taking a chance. Commitments and duties, the demands of family, conflicts of interest with more pressing or 'important' actions, the need to secure regular income, other people's opinions . . . these can all constrain individuals and block their creativity.

The third 'circle of constraint' that Robinson (2009) names is the culture in which the person grew up and operates. Cultural barriers to creativity can include the expected norms of a culture; what is generally permitted and allowed by that culture, which may include beliefs, class systems and educational expectations – boys cannot do ballet, girls need to care for family members, poorer people should not expect too much. In these enlightened times there is an expectation of fairness and equality, yet for some people the cultures in which we are raised not only affect our values and outlook, which may feel controllable, they also shape the ways our bodies and brains function. To change it is necessary to find new ways to have new experiences.

Stages of the creative process

> One very important aspect of motivation is the willingness to stop and to look at things that no one else has bothered to look at. This simple process of focusing on things that are normally taken for granted is a powerful source of creativity.
>
> *Edward de Bono (1992: 46)*

Jesson (2012: 5) summarizes the Five Creative Behaviours that, if followed, would help with becoming more creative:

1   questioning and challenging – why are things the way they are, do they need to be like that?
2   making connections and seeing relationships – assembling familiar ideas and material in new and varied ways
3   envisaging alternatives/seeing things in new ways – imagining and visualizing new concepts, patterns and dreams
4   exploring ideas and keeping options open – generating new and original approaches, being flexible to what arises
5   reflecting critically on ideas and outcomes – evaluating both the manner of working and what is produced.

A similar approach is proposed by Carlile and Jordan (2012: 218), who also use a five-stage process, as follows.

1   Beginning with 'assumptions and attitudes', where does the creator start from, what ideas and beliefs do they work with?
2   The second stage is 'conceptualization' – visualizing what could be, imagining new worlds, new modes of action, bringing into the physical world ideas and concepts from the human imagination.

3   Having found a domain to explore, 'creation of ideas' comes next, a free-thinking session to produce as many divergent ideas as possible, where the wacky are welcomed and the impossible considered. (Of course the process may be guided by the medium; an exploration of a new form of cake might start out wanting to produce something edible, though think of innovative UK chef Heston Blumenthal and the use of such things as slug foam and liquid nitrogen in his cookery.)

4   Stage four involves 'exploration of ideas', testing the ideas created so far, playing with them, seeing what works, or does not.

5   The final stage is the 'evaluation of ideas' or a convergence of ideas from the creation and exploration stages; what works in the way needed, what produces the best result, what is most pleasing?

There are similarities between the ideas of Jesson (2012) and Carlile and Jordan (2012), and the differences are chiefly where Jesson stresses the 'conceptualization' stage – making connections and envisaging alternatives – and Carlile and Jordan the 'creation of ideas' stage. Either approach would work well for most modern situations if followed as a framework. Of course, it could be said that creativity needs no framework, and some believe that creativity is 'natural', but in the atomized, prescribed and controlled world, using a framework helps practitioners work outside their usual boundaries and explore chances, if they want.

Creative adults at play: the Beauty of Play conference

Since 2003 the Ludemos Consultancy has been supporting the Beauty of Play conference; this covers two days of playful discussion about play and playwork, mainly in the open air. A 'conference under canvas', it offers a playful mix of workshops and outdoor activities (Else 2013).

To help with dialogue and free-flowing conversation, delegates camp on site and enjoy communal food, creating spaces for exploration and collaboration as they help people mix and spend time in one another's company. The event happens in the first week of September each year, starting Friday evening and running through to midday on Sunday, attracting a broad range of speakers, first-timers, published authors and playwork theorists. There are many playful activities, discussions, workshops, music, fires and storytelling. The sessions last two hours each; this time gives presenters a chance to explore their ideas more fully, and for delegates to reflect in the moment and on their action; precious time that enriches the experiences, rather than rushing from one activity to the next without full consideration.

Many who participate in this event come back year after year for the valuable opportunity it gives them to play and be creative as adults, rather than simply as adults supporting children's play; they recognize that in order to support play they need to be playful. The event offers a safe space for them to metaphorically let their hair down, and take physical, social and conceptual risks, in order to see what happens. Many delegates comment that they wish they could do this more often than just one weekend in the year; while a lovely thought it is sad that usual practices exclude so much pleasure from the usual working day.

These observations point to the features that make the Beauty of Play event rather a special one, because as well as talking about the processes of play and the theories that confuse them, participants get to play with likeminded people who are curious, intrigued and open to what might be across the *liminal space*, just the 'other side of the threshold'. By being creative in our approach to children's play, we are able to be playful ourselves, which enriches our lives and the lives of the children we are lucky enough to work with.

Questions to help practitioners developing reflective practice

- Chose a reflective tool to use in the next week. Try it for a week then evaluate – what do you like? If nothing then choose another tool, but stick with it for another week and try again.
- Take this further by choosing a model for reflection – e.g. Kolb, Gibbs, Moon, the Integral Play Framework – and apply it to your work. Go through the phases of the model. Do they make sense? What is useful, what not? How can you use the information collected to change your practice or environment?
- In reflection, who is doing the reflecting, you or a different you? Where do these personalities live most of the time; who is in charge, who do you want to be in charge?
- Are you prepared to refocus your attention? Can you choose to be more creative using some of the lessons and approaches described above? Mix ideas up a little: write the stages of creative behaviours on five postcards. Shuffle the cards and follow the first card picked up; work through the cards to see if and how it changes your thinking. Compare your results with your usual approach and see which you prefer.

8

An integrated approach to research

If practitioners are to know whether and how their plans and activities have been successful, they will need to evaluate their practice from time to time. Self-evaluation and reflection have been discussed but practitioners often need to contribute to evaluations of whole systems or approaches to practice, for good practice, to produce evidence for funders or inspectors, for personal study or to help with academic research and perhaps improving practice in the sector. Understanding research methods will be useful for all these reasons.

The Integral Play Framework can help with planning research, offering varied perspectives to complement other approaches. This chapter shows how the Framework has been used successfully as an evaluation tool in a national evaluation of playwork provision, in setting-based research to test the validity of practice, and in the business world to assess the quality of play spaces. Philosophies and approaches to research will be explained, and methods and application issues highlighted and discussed.

Two views of the world

Prior to Descartes (who said 'I think therefore I am'), most people believed that the world was created by God or gods, or arose from the actions of dust/atoms in a random and evolutionary manner. After the Enlightenment – when scientific rationality emerged in the west – two divergent schools of thought emerged: the Rationalists (a view using reason as a source of knowledge or justification) and the Empiricists ('seekers after truth' who believed that experiences through the senses were the ultimate source of all human concepts and knowledge). Put simply, reality as humans know it is either determined by what can be measured as 'fact' through the scientific method and what may be experienced as 'sense' as lived experience. Some people are passionate advocates of one or other, though many people swing between the two extremes, often unconsciously.

These two views have developed along separate lines for more than 200 years, and when doing research rationalists and empiricists have been looking for facts in the world or for understanding experiences; looking for facts results in the Positivist tradition, unravelling experiences is the Interpretivist perspective. However, in recent times it has been realized that while there are benefits to both approaches, each by itself is only a partial view of human reality. Human awareness of the world is both as an object in space that is affected by physical causes *and* subjective, as thinking, emotional people who interpret those experiences. The rational view has allowed us to develop the sciences and mathematics so that we are able to come close to understanding the nature of reality at the atomic and quantum levels, and mathematics is able to predict forces at the boundary of our comprehension. The empirical view has given us belief systems and spiritual practices that bring joy and comfort to many, and more recently psychology, sociology, anthropology and cultural studies as well as other branches of the social sciences, the sciences focusing on human interactions. The Integral Play Framework helps as it incorporates and brings both objective and subjective approaches together. It helps the researcher consider physical attributes, social roles, cultural beliefs, and cognitive and emotional responses.

Positivist and interpretivist approaches

Positivist researchers use methods (experiments/trials/surveys) from the established sciences as tools for understanding the world and things in it by constructing empirically falsifiable theories; taking a position and testing to see if it is correct. Interpretivist researchers (also known as 'anti-positivist') by contrast use social critique or symbolic interpretation (interviews/observations/journals), taking a broad view in order to understand experiences in the context that manifested them. Urie Bronfenbrenner explained the difference quite well when he said that the rationalist, scientific approach resulted in looking at children (our subjects) in unnatural environments, doing unnatural activities for the shortest time; by contrast, the interpretivist study of children in their natural habitats led to Bronfenbrenner's ecological model (1979) based on trying to understand the multiple influences on children's behaviour and moods, including children themselves. In modern research practice, it is common to use multi-modal (multi-method) approaches by, for instance, combining quantitative and qualitative techniques; so when looking at events in children's settings, the frequency of activities may be considered important (a quantitative assessment), yet also what the children did in those activities, and how they or practitioners valued the experience (qualitative assessments). Flick (2006: 229) describes it this way: 'The combination of multiple methodological practices ... adds rigour, breadth, complexity, richness and depth to an inquiry'.

A brief discussion on ethics

When carrying out research on other human beings, children especially, it is recognized that the work must be done to principles that have been agreed over time. Some of these are supported by legislation, others are simply recognized as good practice that protect those involved and help the project run more effectively. Each field had its own version of ethical guidelines and these should be referred to consistently throughout the work if they are to be effective and the work is to be recognized as competent by others.

Research is an additional activity to whatever else the setting or practitioners chose to do; it must therefore do no harm to either participants, staff and parents or the research team themselves. The project should aim to do positive good, it should aim to improve matters, chiefly in this case for playing children or those who support children in their play, rather than simply expose weaknesses in practice or approach. It must therefore respect the individuals and institutions involved, who should be fully informed about the nature and purpose of the research being undertaken – there ought to be few secrets in the modern research project. The research team will be exposed to many 'secrets' about the setting, staff and children they come into contact with, they must respect confidences, wherever possible, referring to the participants and settings in confidential terms in the final write-up, unless specific permission has been obtained from the participants. That caveat, 'wherever possible', is necessary as legislation states that if children disclose matters that should be investigated further, such as matters relating to abuse or harm of some kind, then the investigator is bound by law to take the matter further and report it to the relevant authorities. It is therefore necessary to be honest and truthful, and report what is found objectively and with as little personal comment or bias as can be achieved. And overall the work should strive to improve knowledge and practice if possible, highlighting lessons learned so that others may benefit from the work done.

The ethical code of any research must be used and honoured through all stages of research, planning, data collection, use and storage, write-up, final report, dissemination and close of the project. It is this that must underpin all research work if it is to be recognized as 'true' by the participants, and be authentic and valid to the sector. Not an easy task, but necessary.

Using the Integral Play Framework as a basis for research

The Integral Play Framework helps researchers by bringing together the objective view of the word with the subjective view, and also the personal view with the collective; it thus brings rational views together with subjective interpretations, and individual views with others' views. While each theme may be considered alone, by taking a cross-theme approach, researchers are able to build up a 'rich picture' of data (Denscombe 2003) to get closer to accuracy (*truth*) of the area being investigated.

Looking at children's play activities, there are four main ways to access the situation (see Table 8.1): through the child's self-esteem, community relationships, physical abilities and decision-making opportunities.

Table 8.1 Assessing children's experiences of play.

Self-esteem (self-confidence, identity) could be explored through questions or assessments like:
- What words would you use to describe yourself? This could be assessed with a range of words or images that would be read or shown to children depending on their ability.
- What makes you happy/satisfied, etc.?
- What makes you sad/upset, etc.?

Community relationships (friendships, group connections) could be assessed though interviews with participants or observations of them playing such as:
- Who do children play with?
- Who are their favourite people/best friends?
- Who do they not like/not get on with/choose not to play with?

Physical abilities (using the body to move around or explore the environment) may be more quantitative as occurrences may be counted or assessed using a checklist:
- Where do children play?
- What games do they play?
- How far can they swim/run/walk?

Decision-making opportunities (or relative status in society) may be measured by focusing on:
- Who makes decisions for children?
- Who or what stops them doing the things they want to do?
- What would they like to have a say about?
- If children could have one wish to improve their world/life what would it be?

Looking at children's settings, research may look at children's identities and self-esteem, relationships in the setting, physical resources and decision-making processes.
- How are identity and personality celebrated in the setting? How varied are responses in the setting, how similar?
- How do children value themselves, their friends, their peers and staff in the settings?
- What resources may children use to play? How available are they, how plentiful? Do they change regularly?
- How do children make changes at the setting? How often do staff actively listen to them? Are the decisions tokenistic or do they affect significant changes? Are their decisions used in policy or procedures?

These are simple examples; each theme or area may be explored in depth or the more objective criteria may be exclusively focused on. Other examples will be explained in the case studies below.

Common research tools

Some researchers consider observations the simplest and 'easiest' methods to use, yet like all tools, observations are only as useful as the person applying them. Observations are considered easy because we observe every day, we see things around us all the time and we form judgements about what we see. But for observations to be considered as research they need to be carefully planned with the care applied to any other method. Interviews are useful for collecting the opinions of participants, and literature reviews for collecting the views of experts or authors. Combinations of methods are often used to help form as 'rich' a view as possible of the setting under consideration.

All methods need to be chosen for the type of data they will reveal; observations are not good if the researcher wants to know the view of participants, interviews are not appropriate if they want to see participants' practice. The form of the method should be considered, as each has a different application, uses different techniques and reveals varied factors. The sample of participants should be considered: is the style and depth of the tool one that they can identify with and respond to? If they find it 'hostile' or too invasive they may withdraw from the project. The practicality of the tool should be considered; will it take too long to carry out; will it produce consistent results?

This will be a brief overview of the research process and interested readers should consider some of the many books available dedicated to the process of carrying out field research, writing literature reviews, and identifying methodologies for research and methods for collecting and analysing data.

Literature reviews

A common research tool that is often the start of a research task is that of preparing a literature review, whether library/academic journal based or setting based. The majority of reviews are done using recognized materials such as books, journals and peer-reviewed articles; though on occasion and especially with case studies and action research (see below), it becomes necessary to review documents generated and used within settings. While a literature review is necessary to understand the background in support of field research, it is possible to research simply using literature and the works of others to expose contradictions or similarities across topics and more often across disciplines.

A literature review enables the researcher to position their project within the wider body of work done by other practitioners and researchers, building on their views and supporting or challenging them through the new work carried out. Books, journals and articles (whether paper based or, increasingly, web based) usually cover knowledge that has been accepted by an academic discipline and recognized through the process of peer reviewing as being good enough for publication – though when discussing policy it may be necessary to go to government sources for relevant legislation and guidance, and local sources for setting policy and procedure if they come under the remit of the project. The review should therefore contain ideas that the writer agrees with and those that disagree or question the view taken for the research project. The views expressed should therefore be critical, in two senses of that word: they should be relevant to the subject under investigation, and they ought to expose weaknesses in the idea or thesis used in the overall project so that the thesis may be supported or refuted.

The literature review begins with the lead question of the research project, the subject under investigation. The lead question will normally have three or four sub-questions that clarify the focus of the research and what needs to be investigated. Once clarified, these questions form the backbone of the project and should be kept in mind throughout the duration of the work, which begins with the literature review. The key words in the questions are the ones that set the parameters of the literature search; typically they will include the main theme of the work, the sample group being investigated, the setting in which they operate, the activities under investigation, the law and policy that affects the work, the barriers and supports for such work. For example, a project looking at the effectiveness of the forest school approach for a primary setting would focus on the key topic 'forest schools', yet with a focus on the primary age range of 6–12 years. In looking at effectiveness, good practice would need to be defined and explained. The type of setting would be a secondary theme in the review as the policy and ethos of the setting is likely to affect the approach taken to the topic. The views of practitioners and children are also potentially relevant so local information may need to be investigated. Definitions of key terms, the sample and the setting would all need to be explained to help the reader understand the context under which the research was conducted. The aims of the review would be to make clear the varied opinions relating to the topic, yet end with a clear position of why and how the researcher was carrying out research on the subject at the time of the project. The review should therefore be well written, with a clear beginning, middle and end, supported by referencing that shows where the reader, if needed, may follow up the sources for additional information.

The themes exposed in the review should be those used in the project for data collection, data analysis and then used in the final conclusion; some researchers call this the 'golden thread' that runs through the whole piece. The aim of the researcher should be to stay focused on the main questions and so keep a tight view on the subject being investigated, without too much distraction or straying from the main focus. At the completion of the project there should be a clear explanation of how the project supported or challenged the lead questions and therefore the themes of the research. With an understanding of the theory behind the work, it becomes possible to carry out research using various methods.

Observations

Observations come in several formats, which are explained below. All observations should record the date, time, duration and place of observation, the participants present, their details – age, gender, ability, specific needs – and the person doing the observation. Observations may be digitally recorded, but that method may bring in potential flaws of its own, such as loss of data due to sound levels, confused sounds if several people speak at the same time, and batteries running out, to name a few. Recordings may also miss the most significant factor, the nature of the interaction between participants, the *affect*, their emotion and body language, which may show how words can mean the opposite of actions.

Narrative observations tell the story of what is seen, recording the actions and vocalizations of the target sample; they are often brief – between 5 and 15 minutes in duration. While aiming to be a simple, accurate written record, the speed of activities and speech may lead to errors in data collection unless other precautions are taken, such as recording the observation alongside the written version. When analysing narrative observations a variety of concepts and theories may be used: the role of adults, children's roles and relationships, gender interests, inclusion and exclusion, different areas of engagement (e.g. physical, cognitive, symbolic, emotional, cultural, social), play types, play cues, to name a few.

Time sample observations are good for capturing a longer sequence of events, though may miss intervening detail. Time samples may be carried out for 2 minutes every 5, 10, 15 minutes for an hour or longer period, and may record in the narrative style, or may be focused on specific activities or areas – for example, recording the activities at or near a sand tray or home corner. Problems with time sampling are that, as well as missing significant events, participants may leave the field of research so their actions will not be recorded, hence the need to be clear about the focus of the research: is it about the actions of the participants, or about the use of the setting/environment?

Event observations are a hybrid of narrative and timed observations. If the focus in research was to be on interactions between specific children, or the use of a particular piece of equipment or the behaviour of a named child, then event observations are useful for when the event occurs; as much detail as possible would be recorded, with the emphasis on the type and duration of interactions, actions and affects. Again event observations may not record the actions leading up the event, which may be very significant, though they do record how people act in the specific event. Such observations may be useful for helping plan interventions for when these events occur again, or to help set up environments so that the events are less likely to happen.

Learning stories are a specific form of observation based on the *Te Whariki* curriculum framework from New Zealand, which looks at the learning disposi- tions of the child under observation (Carr 2001). These dispositions look at the cultural, holistic development of the child, and include taking an interest, persisting, questioning, collaborating and taking responsibility. The observa- tions are often recorded in note form much like a narrative observation, then later the practitioner will link the seen actions to the dispositions to categorize what they saw. Such observations may lead to interventions in the environment or with the child, with the aim of offering a new or altered experience for the child, much as in Vygotsky's Zone of Proximal Development (1976).

Tally charts are a more quantitative form of observation, where the aim is to record the incidence of specific activities. Tally charts are useful for recording the frequency of events or to compare different forms of behaviour or activity. If the researcher wanted to record how many children used a specific area of the setting, or to compare two areas – say, an area for general play or an area for den building – then the tally chart would be used over a period of time to record the numbers of children active in the given area. Tally charts may be used for around 10–15 minutes or for 5-minute intervals over a longer period, as with time sampling. Tally charts are good for following the activities of larger sample groups, though the compromise is that detail is lost, the time spent at the activity is not recorded, nor the quality of the activity, unless another research method is used later with the same group. Tally charts are also more positivist in that categories are selected before the observation is carried out; these categories may then be made into a chart to allow for a speedy tick response when the activity is seen. The responses may be compared afterwards by counting frequencies.

Tracking is a method of recording how much time a child spends on an activity. It involves creating a diagram of the space in which the child plays, and then recording the duration and direction of change of the child over a set period, which may be over an hour or longer. Repeat observations will build up a picture of where the child plays and for how long. Tracking is a good tool for recording the areas of the play setting visited by a child/children, the frequency of visits by participants and the use of different areas in a setting. However, tracking is not useful for understanding why children spend time in those areas; to find that out, another method must be used. To track a child a scale drawing should be made of the area under investigation. The usual details about the participants and setting should be recorded. When tracking a child or small group of children (three is a manageable number for one observer), each child should be allocated a code number (e.g. A, B, C), which should be recorded on the tracking sheet/plan along with the start time of the observation. When the child moves to another area, the direction of movement and the time should be recorded by the use of an arrow towards the destination space with the time of arrival (e.g. B → 2.31). At the end of the observation, the sheet will show a series of arrows and times, indicating the child's movement around the space; the time spent at each space may be calculated later.

While observations will collect lots of data about the activities of participants, to find out what they were thinking requires the use of other techniques.

Interviews

Interviews are useful for getting lots of information on the views of participants, their understanding of settings and also their opinions on subjects they have experienced. Interviews allow the researcher to collect lots of detailed data about a child's views and experiences; they are more intimate than many techniques in that they are usually carried out one to one so the researcher can collect information on confidential or sensitive issues, for which the child needs to feel comfortable with the process and the interviewer. If the child feels comfortable the solo interview means that the views of that child are uncovered, whereas in group situations the child may tend to agree with their friends and peers. The data collected is qualitative and may be difficult to interpret as the themes can overlap and be quite interconnected. Interviews are usually of three types: structured, semi-structured and informal.

All types of interview require a similar set-up; a quiet place away from the hubbub of the setting is often needed to help both the researcher and the participant. The room should be comfortable for the interviewee; if they feel threatened or ill at ease it will affect their experience and so the quality of answers received. The researcher should check that the space is suitable beforehand and should check that the participant is happy with the space and the arrangements.

Structured interviews are where the researcher has prepared a series of questions beforehand that they want the participant to answer. The questions should be based around the key themes of the research and the structure encourages responses in line with the themes. While these set questions may help later with transcribing, using themes and with data analysis, they may limit the amount of data collected as the participant is encouraged to stay 'on script' so may self-edit or restrict their answers.

Semi-structured interviews have a loose structure, perhaps with key themes or starting questions, but the interview encourages the participant to add their own views and to 'meander' around the topic. In this way the discussion can reflect more of the participant's own experience, and so becomes more relevant to them, their story. Starting questions should be limited to around five to seven so that the interviewer does not feel too pressured by the process. If the participant is comfortable, the interview may end up being quite extended and running for 30 minutes or longer; if the process is not working, all the questions may be answered in a few minutes. Transcriptions of the interview may then be analysed using the base questions as lead themes, though allowing for others to emerge in the process.

Informal interviews have very little structure, and the topics emerge from the conversation between the researcher and the interviewee. While the informality may be useful for some participants, the lack of structure means that the conversation could range literally anywhere. While the researcher will have the key themes of the research in mind, the lack of structure means they need to rely on memory and perhaps chance for the themes to emerge. And if the interviewee talks more about matters that are relevant to them, then the time in the interview may be spent on matters not relevant to the research. Data analysis will be thematic, though may have more complex themes than with semi-structured interviews.

Interviews and observations are useful when the researcher wants to be in control, and there are other methods that give the participants more of a say about their interests. Like all research these various methods should be paired with other approaches so that the researcher has as complete a view of the topic as possible.

Self-originating material

In parallel to a changing view of childhood (i.e. moving from children being small adults to independent citizens in their own right), some research methods have emerged that respect the views of individual children or participants. These methods include drawings, photos, video, stories and journals, among other methods.

Common to all these methods is that the data was originated by the participant and then shared with the researcher. The need for the data would be discussed with the child, who then decides whether to participate or not; a variety of methods may be offered. The methods are then explained by the researcher, though the content is then determined by the participant, dependent on their understanding of the topic and their confidence in sharing information.

Photos and video are effectively self-observations, with drawings being a memory-reliant 'observation' or psychological projection. The purpose of each is the same: to see the world from the child's point of view. In the digital age there are many ways of creating a static or moving image using electronic media, computers and tablets, as well as pencil, paint and crayon. It is good practice, especially with new technology, to allow the children to become familiar with the tools of research before collecting vital data. It may also be necessary to distribute equipment to all children in a setting so that the participants in research do not feel different to their peers and so that behaviour is as natural as possible. The material generated by non-participants should be honoured and recognized, though should not be used in the study if permissions have not been obtained.

The theme of the research needs to be focused but sufficiently open to encourage clear data collection; e.g. 'my favourite place to play', 'the activity I like best', and so on. Children will generate as many images as they feel comfortable doing in the time. Cameras and videos may generate lots of material in quite a short time; drawings may be single images or a series of images. Several years ago a group of children from a war zone settled in a northern city and the local authority set up a play scheme to help them adjust to life in England. Without prompting, the children's drawings took on symbolism from their recent experiences, often incorporating planes and tanks, exploding buildings, and dead or bleeding bodies. While research material may not be as graphic as these images, it may produce material that is vital to the child and so should not be dismissed as irrelevant or not significant.

Likewise when analysing photos and video, be sure to check the meaning of every image. Often at the outset images may be of the child and their peers pulling faces and performing for the camera; these images may be useful to help define friendship groups. Later on when the 'work' for the research is undertaken, the images may become more formal. It is important to consider all images, usually in an interview or discussion with the participant. In one research project, a child had taken a photograph of an empty wall, the researcher was about to pass on the image when the child explained what it was about. The empty wall represented a favourite activity that was missing, which had been taken away by the staff – in many ways that image became the most poignant of the set.

If the children are skilled enough, then personal stories and journals may be used to record their activity or to comment on events and experiences. These methods will usually generate lots of material of a personal and involved nature, so very useful for some projects where the personal voice is valued, less helpful for 'quick and dirty' research carried out around one topic or lead activity.

Analysis of self-originated material, whether images or stories, may be difficult and time consuming due to the varied and personal nature of the media, though can be very rewarding if the researcher persists. The themes identified are likely to be emergent as the work will have been produced by the participants and not led by the researcher; this gives a valued insight into the child's life so the data will speak to that experience. Of course it then falls to the researcher and practitioners to respond to the messages that the data reveals, so that the research does not become tokenistic, and avoids the participants feeling used and exploited. Even if told that changes cannot be put into practice, that is better than not acknowledging the time and effort that went into contributing to the project. While this is true of all research, it becomes particularly relevant when the child participants have done most of the work themselves.

Action research

Action research is used by researchers who work in the setting in which they want to carry out research; it is an approach that involves examining the practices or people as they occur and change. Action research often requires practitioners investigating and evaluating their own practice to have an emphasis on improving it and making it better; it entails looking at the interconnections of what people value in their work, what they do and how they interact with others. As the researchers are better known by the participants, may be better trusted and so may implement change better, it is considered by some to be more participatory and emancipatory, however, care must be taken not to manipulate or exploit participants. As the work is led by practitioners in their setting rather than academic researchers, it may be harder for others to refuse to participate as they could do with outsiders. And while the approach may create a lot of change in a specific setting, that change may not affect others; due to the intimate and local nature of actions, the implications are not universally applicable.

Action research uses a range of methods that may be quantitative and qualitative according to what it is that the researchers want to uncover. Any of the methods outlined above may be useful to give insights into the process and practices used within the setting. The approach asks that action researchers go through the process of planning, acting and reflecting, focusing on the area of practice under investigation. By identifying possible solutions to issues in the setting, the reflective focus allows practitioners to plan for change and then implement it, seeing what difference it makes. Having assessed the impact of changes, a revised plan is then created to improve on changes, to enhance them or to refocus the action in another part of the setting. The cycle can continue until the process is agreed to participants' satisfaction or the project is completed. In reality the stages may overlap and become more interconnected than is indicated in a simple plan; however the process still has merit provided that the focus remains on critical analysis and documented change. Indeed the greatest contribution of action research over 'good practice' is the rigour applied to implementing new actions and assessing the impact of changes; the approach attempts to be more focused and objective.

The Mosaic Approach and multi-modal methods

Clark and Moss (2001) devised the Mosaic Approach to investigate childhood settings on the premise that children as well as adults had something to say about the practice and culture of the setting. The approach uses different tools, such as observations, role-play, children's drawings, focused group discussions and use of media devices, to form a view of the setting from many perspectives. The adult researcher's role then becomes one of helping the child to make their opinions known, for example by asking questions of the children to elicit their views, or to enhance the images and activities they have been involved in. Clearly this support needs to be sensitively implemented to ensure that the children are saying what they want to say and are not being controlled or manipulated by the grown-ups. While the aim of the Mosaic Approach, like that of action research, is to involve more players and more voices, it can be open to exploitation and corruption unless carefully and conscientiously applied.

Multi-modal methods recognize the complexity and interconnectivity of actions, and aim to find a way to work with them. Like the approaches explained above, multi-modal methods originally used multiple views to arrive at a fuller picture of the topic under discussion. Using differing methods allowed for varied views to be exposed. As the approach has gained credibility and has been critically reviewed, multi-modality has come to mean more than simply an approach to research; it helps shape the thinking behind and the response to research itself.

Not only do differing methods allow for different versions of the 'truth', the different methods allow for it to emerge through different understandings of reality. An overemphasis on academic approaches and language in research has tended to preference those able to understand that language; research has therefore tended to favour cognitive methods and cognitive responses. Those who use multi-modality acknowledge that human experiences are affected by the varied responses of thought and action, mind and body, and by social and cultural interconnections with others, and that these modes have different languages and ways of being. Thus using multi-modes not only permits different methods of data collection but also different ways of understanding and communicating experiences. While this approach facilitates more data and more versions of the experience, it also makes the process of data analysis more interesting in that the intent and meaning of the participants needs to be understood to make meaning of the data. For example, when respondents talk about settings or activities they tend to refer to them as 'mine', inferring ownership or possession, whereas in reality the activity may be communal or belong to another. The researcher would need to be sensitive to these various meanings in order to verify the speaker's intent through further questions or observations. As Merleau-Ponty (1948: 70–72) said, 'It is impossible, in this world, to separate things from their way of appearing . . . Form and content – what is said and the way it is said – cannot exist separately from one another'. This implies that we cannot ultimately know the truth of reality unless we can 'see' every perspective, and while we can strive to be objective about form and content, ultimately the scale of the project will defeat us; we can begin to approach the truth as we understand it but it will remain out of reach. Yet the journey is interesting for what it reveals and for what we find out about ourselves and others along the way; and that alone is enough to give our activities merit.

Using four quadrants in the research field

The Integral Play Framework tool has been used successfully in research to collect data from varied perspectives on three different activities: the evaluation of a national tool for assessing playwork provision, in the business world to assess the quality of play, and in setting-based research to test the validity of practice. Each project used the four quadrants to frame the data collection in order to form a rounded view of the topic. The first example explored will be setting-based research to examine the effectiveness of a practical intervention.

Setting-based research to test the validity of practice: New Games in a primary school

New Games is a well-established approach to cooperative and team games that has been promoted for more than 30 years across the world. However, the effectiveness of the approach had only been appreciated through experience and anecdote, so the promoters of New Games wanted to carry out research in order to assess its impact in a UK primary school. Sheffield Hallam University was approached to do the work and a small team put together to carry out the work (Else *et al.* 2010).

The project made use of the Integral Play Framework (see Figure 2.1) – that is, in order to work with the child physically, it was also recognized that the child's motivation and relationship with others affected their willingness and ability to participate in games. It was proposed that in providing interventions for children's play, the role of the adult was to support children and young people in the creation of games in which they can choose to engage.

Using the model, a series of opportunities for assessing each quadrant of the framework were arrived at (See Table 8.2).

Table 8.2 Integral Play Framework (IPF) quadrant opportunities for assessment.

IPF quadrant	Opportunity
My mind	Expressing satisfaction Feeling enjoyment Problem solving
My body	Running, jumping, balancing Coordinating movements and actions Better general health and reduced obesity
My cultural world	Cooperating with others Respecting beliefs
My social world	Working alone Team activities

A six-month-long intervention using the New Games materials and approaches was planned with a class in a primary school in North Sheffield. The project wanted to show that, through playing New Games, pupils would experience:

- improved coordination and physical ability
- better general health and reduced obesity
- a better self-image, since all will be able to participate successfully in the activities
- better academic performance through flexibility of brain function, creative problem solving and improved learning skills such as listening and following directions
- improved cooperation and respect for others
- better understanding of teamwork skills in a group.

No weighting was made of the elements, nor was an attempt made to say which were mandatory and which optional. From a holistic perspective all the elements should have been present all the time, though it was recognized that this was hard to achieve given resource allocations.

The project followed two classes for a period of 20 weeks; one class did traditional physical activities, the other followed a New Games Curriculum, in which children were never 'out' of the game (i.e. inactive), and which focused on the leadership and involvement of the children. It was expected that pupils in the New Games group would develop a higher motivation to participate, picking up the benefits in the process.

A series of research tools were used in the field to assess the children's experiences, and were developed as a result of that work (see Table 8.3). Comments are made on the effectiveness of the tools.

All tests took place in the school hall or playground and replaced a planned physical activity session. The pupils were in groups of five or six to help keep them motivated (not having to wait too long) and for ease of explanation, which required six researchers to operate the tests, with a supervisor 'fire-fighting' and offering support.

The school hall was a large space, big enough to contain the groups, but the noise levels were difficult at times. Also, privacy was needed to complete the questionnaires, which required taking the pupils into different spaces. One of the tests (coordination using a beat) was found to work better with amplified music. After adaptation many of the tests worked well though the results dependent on teacher support were incomplete, again due to the difficulty of implementing alongside other class activities (i.e. priority was given to established routines rather than the research).

Table 8.3 New Games research tools

Opportunity	Assessment	Tool
Expressing satisfaction Feeling enjoyment	A better self-image was to be measured through the use of guided questionnaires with children	Guided questionnaires with children (using relevant questions from Table 8.1 – *Assessing children's experiences of play*)
Cooperating with others Respecting beliefs	Improved cooperation and respect for others was assessed through questionnaires and teacher observations	Guided questionnaires with children Teacher observations (using an agreed format)
Running, jumping, balancing Coordinating movements and actions	Improved coordination and physical ability was tested through ABC activities: Agility, Balance and Coordination	Two tests: • balance test (walking slowly along a low-level balance beam) • coordination (bouncing and catching a ball in time to a metronome beat)
Better general health and reduced obesity	Better general health and reduced obesity was to be assessed through a simple health check using objective criteria	Due to ethical considerations, the planned health check was replaced with an agility-based stamina test (running between a series of five cones, 10 m apart, for 1 minute's duration)
Working alone Team activities	Better understanding of teamwork skills was assessed through researcher observations	Researcher observations of intervention programme (using the agreed format)
Problem solving	Better academic performance	Teacher reports (using standard academic formats)

However, the project showed that assessing using the four quadrants of the Integral Play Framework was possible and practical. The work showed a small but significant benefit was gained by the target group who were involved in the New Games Approach: they showed an improvement in their stamina over the period of the programme; this improvement was more marked in target group boys who did better than control boys. In the tests for coordination and balance, target group girls did better than control group girls. Teachers were asked to comment on classroom behaviour as a result of the programme. Class teachers reported that cooperation was 'Much better' as a result of the programme.

The most significant benefits were noted for individuals, for whom teachers reported key changes. Examples included an overweight pupil who had felt excluded from games and who, at the end of the study, was more active, better involved with their peer group and more willing to join in active games sessions. Another pupil was assessed to have a 'more positive attitude towards others and more willing to talk about problems'. Overall it was considered that the use of the Framework had been successful in capturing a fuller, more rounded part of the children's experiences of the New Games activity.

Evaluation of a national quality assurance scheme for playwork provision: *Quality in Play*

In 2010, Play England commissioned an evaluation of the impact of *Quality in Play (QiP)* (NCB 2008), a quality assurance scheme for out-of-school play and childcare provision to ensure quality play opportunities for children.

In order to gain *QiP* accreditation, providers contact the national agency, Play England, to register for the scheme. Providers then work through each quality area in the *QiP* manual, ensuring that policies and procedures are up to date, documents easily accessed, and that standards of good practice are in place on site. Most settings work with a mentor to help them through the process. Settings could choose to purchase the support of a mentor (trained by Play England) or not as they wished; some used experienced staff as internal mentors. (The internal approach worked very well in one large authority, where the mentor supported sites on a regular basis through meetings and training sessions.) Evidence is collected in a portfolio for review during the *QiP* assessment. The *QiP* assessor then visits the site to discuss the contents of the portfolio and observe how staff interact with children. The assessor prepares a report based on their visit, which is sent to the provider for agreement, along with requests for any further information required before accreditation could be granted. An independent *QiP* panel reviews the assessments to decide whether to grant accreditation. Once accredited, the *QiP* team sends a certificate to the successful setting for them to display on site. Accreditation is valid for a period of two years, though a move to three years was being considered as part of the continuous revision of the *QiP* manual. The scheme is therefore holistic and covers many areas of the setting's work, its approach to children, and its practices and procedures.

The *QiP* evaluation commission was offered to Ludemos Associates, which used the Integral Play Framework to help assess the *QiP* process; the approach is outlined in Table 8.4. Data was identified in four different types using the domains of the Framework, prior to field research, data analysis and write-up in the report, *A Journey Not A Destination* (NCB 2010).

For clarity of data collection, five lead research themes were considered, four using the Framework and the fifth on the process of the *QiP* evaluation. These were matched to the *QiP* portfolio evaluation criteria to help practitioners make the connection to the research process, i.e. using terms they were familiar with from *QiP* – see Table 8.5.

Using these themes, a series of questions was prepared to investigate the direct provision for children's play, settings' resources and their policies, and the connection to the wider community and other agencies. The full set of questions was shown in the final report on this project, *A Journey Not A Destination* (NCB

Table 8.4 The approach to data collection used in the *Quality in Play* research.

Types of data	Methods of field research: assessing the holistic work of the setting	
Internal context: setting procedures, documents and portfolios, practice changes	Document review	
On-the-ground provision, human and environmental	Observations and interviews Witness testimony	
Practitioners', managers', parents' and users' impressions and views	Interviews Witness testimony	**Which overall led to →** **Outcomes: Highlighting the changes as a result of QiP**
External context; stakeholder perspectives, changes for children's play in the wider community	Document review Interviews Witness testimony	

Table 8.5 Linking research themes to the *Quality in Play* criteria.

Research themes	QiP criteria v4
The experience of the *QiP* process	
Practice and the quality of provision for children's play	Children's Freedom and Control Reflective Playwork Practice Communicating Effectively Clear Play Aims and Values The Human Play Environment The Physical Play Environment
Organizational standards for the provider	Project and Resource Management Workforce Development The Law and Regulation
The engagement of providers with the wider community	Working in the Community
Working with other agencies	The Bigger Picture

2010). In addition to observations of the settings and their resources, interviews were held with managers, supervisors, staff and partners for 13 settings nationwide, covering a variety of types of setting, including schools, adventure playgrounds, afterschool cubs and training organizations. Additional information was collated from reports and reviews before and after the *QiP* assessment, portfolio evidence for the *QiP* assessment, including photos and other evidence, as well as results from consultation with children and young people.

The full results were included in the Final Report (NCB 2010); the two main views reported by participants were that *QiP* had made a difference to their practice. The first was that *QiP* had validated current practice and highlighted areas where settings could make improvements in order to work towards good practice. It had given participants confidence to believe in their practice, and make the case arguing for its existence and development. The second was that it had led to a wholesale review of providers' practice and had led to changes on the ground that had fundamentally improved children's access to freely chosen play opportunities. As the review was holistic and covered many aspects of their work, this had led to step-changes in practice and attitudes in the settings towards children and their play; 'The benefits were greatest for those settings who were fully subscribed to the quality assessment process and were prepared to reflect wholeheartedly on their practice and on themselves' (NCB 2010: 4).

One example given in the report was from a setting manager who had previously been qualified in early years work, and by her own admission had a tentative approach to children making their own choices in play. The manager referred to what she called a 'light bulb moment' when she realized that children could take self-managed risks in their play supported by skilled staff. That realization had led her to more and deeper reflection (of the kind discussed in Chapter 7) on her work:

> Things changed for me that day. Children will take risks and how are they going to learn if they don't take risks? Kids now put the programme together. I was thinking I couldn't do [the *QiP*] again but in fact it was better . . . Because we had done it before, I learnt from my mistakes and I was updating the existing evidence, adding to it. We are a lot better at gathering evidence; better at reflecting and looking at our work practice. I knew I did my job but I had no evidence of it. There was very little reflection in the past. We now have substantial evidence to back it up.
>
> *NCB (2010: 13–14)*

Overall, the findings of the work (NCB 2010: 4) showed that, though many staff considered *QiP* to be additional work at the beginning, it was also useful evidence for funders and inspectors – and for building staff confidence in their practice, knowing what they were doing and why. The process was considered better if treated as one for continual improvement; it was found to be easier and better the second time around. Staff who had experience of other quality assurance systems and portfolio building found the process relatively easy to complete, due to the clarity of the themes.

Commenting on the use of the Integral Play Framework as a research tool, the research team found the framework helped make sense of the *QiP* criteria and link them in a logical, holistic manner (see Tables 8.4 and 8.5). The four domains, or quadrants, were simple enough for clarity, yet comprehensive enough to allocate all the criteria a place. The approach also focused on the linked but different experiences of children, setting staff, stakeholders and supporters in the wider network. Such an approach helped the people involved in the settings and in the national agency recognize the contributions (and weaknesses) across the project, and so take action where most needed. Traditional research methods may have focused on process systems or setting outputs and so missed some of the personal experiences so vital to changing practice, and so children's day-to-day events.

Assessing the quality of play spaces: *Simply Play*

The final example of the Integral Play Framework in research is in a business setting, working with Timberplay Ltd, a UK-based specialist in children's play spaces offering natural outdoor wooden play equipment (manufactured by its partner Richter Spielgerate), which also offers design advice on hard and soft landscaping, equipment installation and maintenance.

Timberplay approached Sheffield Hallam University through a Knowledge Transfer Project, where industry partners work with universities to apply theory in business settings, originally with an idea to create an evaluation tool for the assessment of play environments. As discussions exposed more interest in playful approaches, the project also included embedding creative methods for product enhancement, and developing the company's business services in order potentially to influence public policy through the work of the company director. A side project of helping make the company more playful was also adopted. A contract was agreed and the two-year programme started with the recruitment of a Creative Play Associate to manage the project, working within the company but jointly supervised and employed through the university.

To evaluate the play environments, it was agreed to use the framework from 'Maximising play value' (Else, 2008), a working paper that Timberplay and Sheffield Hallam University had explored together previously. Using a version of the Integral Play Framework, the paper set out an approach to providing for play opportunities and the kinds of experiences that children should access from a play space (the model is reproduced in Figure 8.1). For example, the external, personal world or quadrant is where children can run, jump and balance, using their bodies. The internal, personal domain is where they feel enjoyment and solve problems. The shared internal, cultural quadrant could be about playing with identity, and the external shared world is about cooperating with others in their play. An additional six elements covered themes common to all types of play: creative adaptations, changing the environment for play, taking opportunities for risk and challenge, experiencing variety, having sufficient space for the activity, and with adequate support, whether through on-site staff or others, e.g. community wardens or maintenance staff.

These 18 themes were then developed into questions to be used to assess an environment to see if and how well it met the criteria. The elements shown in the model were translated into play value assessments, as shown in Table 8.6. Each play value element was given detail to allow for a scoring of the separate features. The scoring range was from 0 = absent to 4 = excellent. This example shows 'Experiencing the elements and the world' from the external, personal quadrant.

The original model contained 30 questions, though as the project progressed, this developed into 50 questions, following a meta-analysis of several other evaluation systems (e.g. *Best Play* Objectives, NPFA/CPC/ Playlink 2000; CABE Space Inclusive Design 2004; Fields in Trust *Planning and Design for Outdoor Sport and Play* 2008; *Quality in Play* criteria 2008) carried out by the Creative Play Associate. The meta-analysis indicated that the model was valid and encompassed many of the features of the other assessment models, yet in a holistic manner. The analysis also exposed the

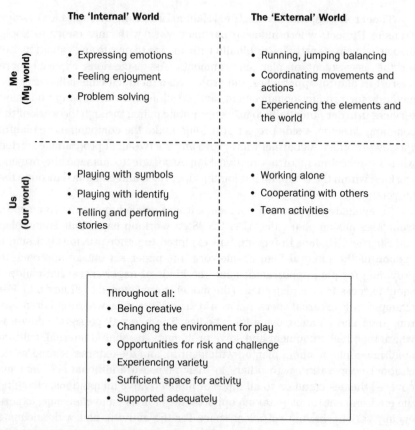

Figure 8.1 Providing opportunities for children's play.

Table 8.6 Play value assessments – example: 'Experiencing the elements and the world'.

Play value element	Assessment				
Experiencing the elements and the world					
Access to the natural elements:	Absent	Limited	OK	Good	Excellent
1. Water – Access and opportunity	0	1	2	3	4
2. Fire – Access and opportunity	0	1	2	3	4
3. Air – Access and opportunity	0	1	2	3	4
4. Earth – Access and opportunity	0	1	2	3	4
5. Stimulation for the senses; different sounds, smells and textures	0	1	2	3	4

additional features that crept into others' 'play assessment', such as safety surfacing, seating, cleanliness, and so on. However, after piloting this tool it was recognized that those features, while they supported the space, did not support play in the way that, for example, access to the natural elements did. The additional features were considered and then rejected for the model, which appropriately was named *Simply Play*, as that is what it focused on.

The *Simply Play* assessment tool was further tested in the field by the Associate, working with designers, maintenance staff, admin staff and customers – the people engaging Timberplay's services. Despite the differing expertise of the participants in carrying out play evaluations, it was found that the tool worked well in that most people understood the criteria without too much explanation, and the Associate was always able to fill in detail if needed. The subjective nature of the assessments meant that scores did not always tally if carried out by several assessors, however the strengths and weaknesses of a site were always apparent and consistent, thus enabling planning for improvements to help offer better play opportunities for children. For example, while the assessors might not agree on whether the challenge present in the space was *good* or *excellent*, they would agree on the presence of challenge in that space. When the total assessment was created, the themes with the best and worst scores would be revealed and so could be used to identify good and better play spaces, and where improvements may be made to help meet children's play needs. For while it is recognized that children can and do play everywhere, they will play more and more creatively when the environment is supportive and with many and varied play choices. While there is a need in the modern world for play spaces – *compensatory spaces*, as Hughes (2012) has named them – adults as providers of such spaces should work to make them the most supportive types of space possible; *Simply Play* helps with that task.

After further refinement and responding to feedback from the pilot that some criteria were too similar to assess separately, the 50 questions were reduced to 45. The original criteria wordings were clarified where needed, the scoring system retained, and new detail added, as well as a comments section to help answer assessors' questions about what to look for (see Table 8.7). Given that many assessors of the play space are play-workers, funders or parent supporters with varied experience of the features of play spaces, it was considered important that the tool be as accessible as possible. Originally designed on paper, as the project progressed it was decided to make the assessment tool available as an online web application, accessible by PC and hand-held tablet or smartphone; that way assessors would be able to enter scores in the field while walking around the play site.

In the final online version, the *Simply Play* tool (accessible from http://www.simplyplay.org.uk) gave access randomly to 45 questions grouped into

Table 8.7 *Simply Play* assessments – example: 'A varied and interesting physical environment'.

Theme/criteria	Scoring	Comments
A varied and interesting physical environment		
Sited on land of varied topography or landscaped for varied play experiences	0—1—2—3—4	How varied is the landscape (bits and pieces) and topography (lumps and bumps) of this space?
Choice of manufactured and natural materials	0—1—2—3—4	Rate the range of materials, both natural and manufactured here
Sub-theme: newness and change		
Things to use (tools/materials)/move around (loose parts)	0—1—2—3—4	How much can the space be changed by those playing? How many objects or tools are there to use?
Opportunities to manipulate natural/fabricated materials	0—1—2—3—4	How varied are the opportunities to manipulate natural and man-made materials in this space?

ten integrated themes. On completion of the assessment, an infograph of the total scores for the site was sent to the assessor, if they wished. The infograph offered a visual representation as well as a percentage score of the sub-total for each theme (see Figure 8.2). As part of the project, it was decided to make the tool freely available to anyone who wanted to use it, the aim being to promote use of the tool and themes and to support the improvement of play value as widely as possible. Evaluation of the tool and feedback from users has been overwhelmingly positive.

The *Simply Play* assessment, like the other two evaluations described above, showed how the Integral Play Framework may be used to help create a holistic view of children's play that comes close to capturing several of the key opportunities for playing, which are different for each child, pleasurable, timeless and a whole body/mind experience. By using a balanced model the aim was to create a view of the world that covers external objectivity with internal subjectivity. We cannot ultimately know the truth of reality as we are

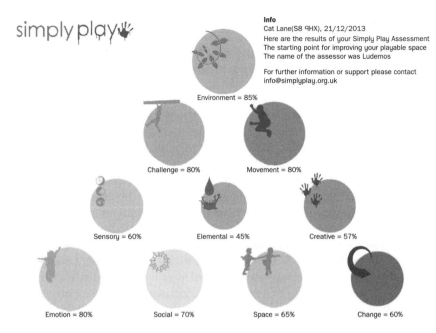

Figure 8.2 *Simply Play* infograph.

living in it. What it means for our work with playing children is that we should try to be objective, or if being subjective that we are clear about what we are commenting on.

Ultimately, our challenge will be to find out if we got it right. *Simply Play* is about evaluating an environment for play, and we have help in seeing if we got it right – the children will let us know through their delight in their play. Children will always make sense of their play if it is self-chosen, engaging and satisfying, for it will be pleasurable and will mean something to them so that they repeat or extend the play. If we get it wrong and children do not feel enjoyment in a space, they will soon let us know.

Making sense of it all

This chapter, and this book, have aimed to describe the tools to be used in offering as wide a range of experiences to children as is possible from the human and physical realities in which they play; it is a challenge, but to do any less may lead to play deprivation and unhappy children. Yet moments of play give joy and pleasure to children, and those collectively lead to children's well-being; performing an activity immersed in a feeling of energized focus, full involvement and enjoyment in the process of an activity is good for children.

Play is pleasurable for each child; it gives enjoyment, satisfaction and 'fun' in the moment of playing – it is a valued part of childhood, perhaps the defining quality of childhood. Play is the way humans develop efficient brains; when children play, the nerve signals the body generates create neural pathways that help with brain development and brain plasticity (flexibility); playing contributes to developing 'effective systems for learning' rather than particular learning outcomes. Playing is a child's free, open, boundless, and self-controlled activity; through play children discover the differences between themselves, others and the world in which they live. These discoveries help them become individuals, independent, self-sufficient and autonomous. Play is chaotic and transformative; it helps children to be spontaneous, highly creative, original and open. Playing connects to 'threshold experiences' and opens up 'worlds of possibility' that children recognize as mysterious and 'magical'. Humans describe play as a right to be promoted and protected, yet it is fundamentally more important than that, and cannot be reduced to a set menu or curriculum; play will emerge everywhere given the right conditions – playing is when we become most alive and most human. And so supporting many opportunities to play makes perfect sense; in childhood and throughout life, we should keep playing.

Questions to help practitioners evaluate effectively

- Spend an hour using the *Simply Play* assessment tool (accessible from http://www.simplyplay.co.uk) to evaluate a play space that you know. Did the results surprise you? What features would you choose to change? How useful was the tool? Would you share the results with a colleague?
- Do you have a specific topic of play that interests you? Could you set yourself a goal of writing an information guide for your colleagues, or for parents in a setting that you know? Can you spend an hour searching the internet for relevant articles or books? Do you have access to a university library where you could check out the latest books on your topic? Write up your findings and seek feedback on what you produce.
- What do you think of the Integral Play Framework as a tool for research; does it work for you? Could you use the four domains, or quadrants, to frame your own research? Could you use or adapt one of the three evaluation systems described to a project that you know well, assessing the environment, an activity or the overall provision?

Appendices

Appendices

Appendix 1
Comparison of definitions of play

In the Summary column are the *Essential Characteristics of Play* as described in this book. Definitions were ascribed to the characteristics as closely as possible (though some are admittedly a little tenuous); the last three items were not used as they are descriptions of outcomes rather than what is happening for the child as they play. Results are spread over two tables as a number of sources were used. The majority of the sources cited as 2011 were taken from the UK magazine *Ip-Dip*, which asked the authors to comment on play in its November and December 2011 issues.

Summary	Garvey (1977)	Playwork Principles (PPSG 2005)	Bekoff (Ip-Dip 74 2011)	Bruce (2001)	Brown (Ip-Dip 75 2011)	Burghardt (Ip-Dip 74 2011)	Cohen (Ip-Dip 75 2011)	Else (2009)	Frost (Ip-Dip 75 2011)
Play is a process, not a thing		Play is a process							
Self-chosen, willingness to participate	Play is spontaneous and voluntary	Play is freely chosen		Children choose to play and cannot be made to play	Directed by the player, voluntary	Relaxed field		A sense of control	
Active engagement, attentive response to feedback	Play involves some active engagement on the part of the player	Play is personally directed			Continuity of desire (looking for ways of keeping it going, i.e. 'handicapping')	Repeated performance		Choice for the player Immediacy of action and response	
Sufficiently safe, physically and psychologically									
A whole body/ mind experience		Play is fundamental to the healthy development and well-being of individuals and communities	Essential for good health					Children need to be active through their play and especially so outdoors	A survival mechanism, essential for health, fitness and well-being

				Provides freedom from the relentlessness of time's arrow	Structural or temporal difference	Timeless – 'in the moment'	
Timelessness, lost in the moment							
Neophilic; attracted to newness or new experience – pretence	Play has certain systematic relations to what is not play		Children rehearse the future in their role-play Children pretend when they play		Elements of make believe		
Neophilic; attracted to newness or new experience – boundary testing		The way in which human and non-human animals learn what's right and what's wrong . . .	Children playing will be deeply involved and difficult to distract from their deep learning; they 'wallow' in their learning		Boundary testing		An inherent propensity to explore, inquire and learn

(Continued)

Summary	Garvey (1977)	Playwork Principles (PPSG 2005)	Bekoff (Ip-Dip 74 2011)	Bruce (2001)	Brown (Ip-Dip 75 2011)	Burghardt (Ip-Dip 74 2011)	Cohen (Ip-Dip 75 2011)	Else (2009)	Frost (Ip-Dip 75 2011)
Neophilic; attracted to newness or new experience – creativity				Children try out their most recent learning, skills and competencies when they play Children make up rules as they play, and so keep control of their play Children use the first-hand experiences that they have in life Children make play props	Provides improvisational potentials	Limited immediate function	Creative	Children's play is influenced by cultural elements . . . they construct their own view of the world and explore things in their play that some adults might disapprove of	

Pleasurable	Play is pleasurable, enjoyable		Serious business but lots of fun		Inherent attraction . . . (fun)		Usually fun		A drive for pleasure and mastery
Different for each person								Players play for their own reasons	
Satisfaction is self-defined with no extrinsic goals	Play has no extrinsic goals	Play is intrinsically motivated		Children when playing have a personal agenda	Appears purposeless (done for its own sake, has intrinsic value)	Endogenous component		Accom-plishment is self-defined	
			Essential for young animals of all species						What children are wired to do and need to do but often find adults in the way
Play is a biological necessity		Play is a biological necessity	Perhaps the most important behaviour in which human and non-human animals engage						An essential element like breathing and eating – but more complex

(Continued)

Summary	Garvey (1977)	Playwork Principles (PPSG 2005)	Bekoff (Ip-Dip 74 2011)	Bruce (2001)	Brown (Ip-Dip 75 2011)	Burghardt (Ip-Dip 74 2011)	Cohen (Ip-Dip 75 2011)	Else (2009)	Frost (Ip-Dip 75 2011)
Play is a psychological necessity		Play is a psychological necessity						Children play with thoughts and feelings	
Play is a social necessity		Play is a social necessity		Children make sense of their relationships with their family, friends and culture				Through play children relate to others	
				Children play alone sometimes					
				Children play together, in parallel, associatively or cooperatively in pairs or groups					

Summary	Huizinga (1950)	Hughes and King (1984)	Kilvington (Ip-Dip 75 2011)	Lester and Russell (2010)	Mainemelis and Ronson (2006)	Pellegrini (Ip-Dip 75 2011)	Russell (Ip-Dip 75 2011)	Rogers (1961)
Play is a process, not a thing		Play is a process – it's the way of playing that is important; not what we play with						
Self-chosen, willingness to participate	All play is a voluntary activity	Play is freely chosen by the player				It's voluntary (an important motivational component)		Freedom of symbolic expression
Active engagement, attentive response to feedback		Play is personally directed; the manner of playing is decided by the child	A means of feeling fully alive	Children's play represents a primary form of participation, being interwoven into everyday life				Personal responsibility
Sufficiently safe, physically and psychologically								Accepting the individual Understanding empathetically

(Continued)

Summary	Huizinga (1950)	Hughes and King (1984)	Kilvington (Ip-Dip 75 2011)	Lester and Russell (2010)	Mainemelis and Ronson (2006)	Pellegrini (Ip-Dip 75 2011)	Russell (Ip-Dip 75 2011)	Rogers (1961)
A whole body/ mind experience				Play is essential to children's health and well-being				
				Play acts across several adaptive systems to contribute to health, well-being and resilience Play can help to mitigate the effects of severe stress				
Timelessness, lost in the moment					Exploring boundaries in time and space			
Neophilic; attracted to newness or new experience – pretence			Essential non-essential behaviour (necessary involvement in the unnecessary)	Play offers opportunities to move beyond existing ways of being, to transform structures and cross borders	Uncertainty/ freedom constraints		'As if' (appropriating aspects of children's known worlds)	

Neophilic; attracted to newness or new experience – boundary testing	It creates order				It's not immediately functional	The deliberate creation of uncertainty – 'in control of being out of control' (Gordon 2007)
Neophilic; attracted to newness or new experience – creativity	It promotes social groupings which are different from the common world	Freedom for the brain to work in a creative, random, quirky, flexible, deep, redundant way when not involved in the mainstream of life / A way of subverting real life	Play is about creating a world in which, for that moment, children are in control and can seek out uncertainty in order to triumph over it	Threshold experiences		
Pleasurable	It has a tendency to be beautiful	A process of thinking, feeling and/or doing, with anticipation of pleasure	Play is primarily behaviour for its own sake, for the pleasure and joy of being able to do it	Positive affect		A way of rearranging the world in a way that makes it either less scary or less boring

(Continued)

Summary	Huizinga (1950)	Hughes and King (1984)	Kilvington (Ip-Dip 75 2011)	Lester and Russell (2010)	Mainemelis and Ronson (2006)	Pellegrini (Ip-Dip 75 2011)	Russell (Ip-Dip 75 2011)	Rogers (1961)
Different for each person	It contains its own course and meaning						A disposition manifest through behaviour and activity	
Satisfaction is self-defined with no extrinsic goals		Play is engaged in for its own sake; the impulse comes from within			Loose association between means and ends	Means over ends are stressed (it is not goal oriented)	Emergent and unpredictable	A climate where external evaluation is absent
Play is a biological necessity				The experience of play effects changes to the architecture of the brain . . .				
Play is a psychological necessity				. . . particularly in systems to do with emotion, motivation and reward				
Play is a social necessity								

One writer, Gordon Sturrock (*Ip-Dip 75* 2011), stated that play has only one function:

> Play does not have many definitions/functions: it has only one. It is a singularity. The sole purpose of play is to induce PLAYING.
>
> Playing is infinite and can be understood only by one factor. That is its boundedness. All of the stuff quoted is actually and merely a description of a particular containment/frame: call it what you will. Approached by an observer outside of the event, playing will be seen as either particular [or procedural]: that is, particle or wave; to that extent it is 'quarky' (to mint a word). The only practical approach (in my opinion) is to take a view that is summed up by asking, at any given moment: what is it that this playing is?
>
> People say, 'It is un-definable but that doesn't mean that we can't say what it is.' In effect you allow playing to play through you and from that intimate interplay arrive at a description and or insight and derive meanings that can be cultivated as a field of such shared insights. Remember the dictum of Sallust on the purpose of myth; he said: 'These things never happened but they are forever.' Or Miles Davis, 'Don't play what's there. Play what's not there.'
>
> We witness deep *koans* of playing and the reduction to language has the possibility of both capturing and missing its essence.

Appendix 2
An expanded taxonomy of play types

After reading many sources on human development and play, Bob Hughes has described play types as the different behaviours seen when children are playing (1996a, 2002). The list is useful to help identify behaviour in order to comment on it and support it in provision.

Hughes originally identified 15 play types (1996a) and then added 're-capitulative play' in 2002 to make 16. As discussed in the main text, it could be argued that there are many hundreds of types of play; or that there are only three basic types. The definitions of Hughes' play types are as follows; the definitions in italics are other play types suggested by the Integral Play Framework (based on other authors' work and experience with playing children), bringing the total of play types in this list up to 27.

Communication play

Play using words, nuances or gestures. For example, mime, jokes, play acting, mickey taking, singing, debate, poetry.

Creative play

Play that allows a new response, the transformation of information, awareness of new connections, with an element of surprise. For example, enjoying creation with a range of materials and tools for its own sake.

Creative cognitive play

Making concepts that that did not exist before for the player, playing with ideas. For example, odd word combinations, puns, making up fantastic creatures.

Creative artistic play

Playing creativity in any of the arts – music, painting, modelling, story-telling, etc. – making things that have never been seen, heard or experienced before by the playing child.

Deep play

Play that allows the child to encounter risky or even potentially life-threatening experiences, to develop survival skills and conquer fear. For example, leaping on to an aerial runway, riding a bike on a parapet, balancing on a high beam.

Dramatic play

Play that dramatizes events in which the child is not a direct participant. For example, presentation of a TV show, an event on the street, a religious or festive event, even a funeral.

Emotional play

Play that is carried out for the emotional feeling generated or to create an emotional effect. For example, watching or interacting with the fall of rain or snow, leaves on a tree, another face or a sunset, pretending to be hurt or happy, angry or elated – a precursor to acting out emotions.

Exploratory play

Play to access factual information consisting of manipulative behaviours such as handling, throwing, banging or mouthing objects. For example, engaging with an object or area and, either by manipulation or movement, assessing its properties, possibilities and content, such as stacking bricks.

Family play

Play relating to the child's immediate family, such as sticking out a tongue, peek-a-boo, tickling, etc., games that initially would not be tolerated if carried out with others, or may create quite a different response, e.g. fear. Family play is a precursor to communication and social play.

Fantasy play

Play that rearranges the world in the child's way, a way that is unlikely to occur in reality for the child. For example, playing at being a pilot flying around the world or the owner of an expensive car.

Global play

This is play that is spontaneous, highly creative, original and open; that unites and identifies with the play of the world (Gordon and Esbjorn-Hargens 2007). It is play that improvises and plays with and beyond roles and relationships, 'crazy wisdom' or trickster play, uniting chaos and order.

Group play

Play relating to the child's immediate friendship group, cliques, gangs, etc. Behaviour that is permissible with a select few but not with the wider community, where the rules are set and agreed by the group.

Imaginative play

Play where the conventional rules, which govern the physical world, do not apply. For example, imagining you are, or pretending to be, a tree or ship, or patting a dog that isn't there.

Impulsive play

Playing on impulse with no concern for the consequences. For example, initially with smaller children, reaching for things, exploring without regard for safety or security, leading to doing things on impulse, with no conscious thought, just a desire to experience, or 'be'. A possible foundation of deep play.

Locomotor play

Movement in any and every direction for its own sake. For example, chase, tag, hide and seek, tree climbing.

Mastery play

Control of the physical and affective ingredients of the environments. For example, digging holes, changing the course of streams, constructing shelters, building fires.

Object play

Play that uses infinite and interesting sequences of hand–eye manipulations and movements. For example, examination and novel use of any object, e.g. cloth, paintbrush, cup.

Perceptual play

Interacting with the world though perceptions of light, sound, smell, heat/ cold, wind. Children's first playful interactions are through basic perceptions and so lead on to being stimulated by the play of light or the sound of waves on a beach, or wind through trees.

Recapitulative play

Play that is a recap of aspects of collective human evolutionary history. For example, rituals, fire making, den/cave making, using weapons, caring for other species.

Role-play

Play exploring ways of being, although not normally of an intense personal, social, domestic or interpersonal nature. For example, brushing with a broom, dialling a telephone, driving a car.

Rough and tumble play

Close-encounter play that is less to do with fighting and more to do with touching, tickling, gauging relative strength, discovering physical flexibility and the exhilaration of display. For example, playful fighting, wrestling and chasing where the children involved are obviously unhurt and giving every indication that they are enjoying themselves.

Sexual play

Playing and exploring sex roles and sexual body parts and functions. For example, 'cross-dressing' as a young child, but also self-touching and exploration of others, leading to 'I'll show you mine . . .' and pubescent fumbling.

Social play

Play during which the rules and criteria for social engagement and interaction can be revealed, explored and amended. For example, any social or inter- active situation that contains an expectation on all parties that they will abide by the rules or protocols, i.e. games, conversations, making something together.

Socio-dramatic play

The enactment of real and potential experiences of an intense personal, social, domestic or interpersonal nature. For example, playing at house, going to the shops, being 'mothers and fathers', organizing a meal or even having a row.

Symbolic play

Using symbols in play to represent other 'real' objects. This play supports children's control, gradual exploration and increased understanding, without the risk of being out of their depth. Examples include using a piece of wood to symbolize a person, or a piece of string to symbolize a wedding ring.

Symbolic conceptual play

Playing with thoughts and concepts in one's head. For example, strategizing for chess or online games, making up mathematical formulae; visualization, seeing things that have never existed before.

Symbolic archetypal play

Playing with and against archetypes, behaving as heroes and villains, magicians and monsters, gods and goddesses. Such play may be conscious or unconscious, and may lead on to full dramatic play, or may be self-contained.

Appendix 3
Psycholudic terminology

The following table explains key terms and phrases used in *psycholudics*, 'the study of the mind and psyche at play', aiming to describe the process of play as it happens (Sturrock, as cited in Sturrock and Else 1998).

Many of these terms were first described by Gordon Sturrock and Perry Else (1998) in 'The playground as therapeutic space: playwork as healing', known as 'the Colorado paper'. Additions were made in 2004 with *Towards Ludogogy: Parts I, II and III* (Gordon Sturrock, Wendy Russell and Perry Else 2004). Other terms have been borrowed from other writers and acknowledgements are given where needed.

Term	Definition
Adulteration	Adulteration occurs when the adult dominates or takes over a child's play for their own purposes, whether those purposes are conscious (working to educational or safety standards) or unconscious (fear, embarrassment, domination).
Æffect	A combination of affect, emotion as used in psychology, and the idea of effect, an outcome or aftermath. So, æffect is emotion or feelings and their outcome or expression seen as a whole; the impact of emotion on a situation. Sturrock (1996)
Affect	Affect is the emotional material, mood or mask that people display. The affect may be 'real' or 'false'; in playing, children may play with affect as part of their emotional development. This may then have an effect on those around them – see also **Æffect**.

(Continued)

Term	Definition
Annihilation	Play annihilation is the end of the play for the child at that time.
	This may be a simple end to the game or a dramatic destruction of the model or sandcastle they have spent an hour carefully constructing. Annihilation will occur when the play frame has no more meaning for the child, when the child has got whatever they were looking for from the play experience. Adults working with children can often misunderstand this. Adults/workers can be dismayed when a piece of art, instead of being mounted and displayed on the wall, is painted over and thrown in the bin. Annihilation is about the child taking their choice in the play to a natural conclusion.
Association and amplification	The associative playwork task may be to 'make ample' the imagery, ideas and symbols of the child's enacted play. By extending our own knowledge, workers are able to help children from all cultures with playful expression.
	'Amplification involves the use of mythic, historical and cultural parallels in order to clarify and make ample the metaphorical content of [the play] symbolism.' Based on Samuels *et al.* (1986) *A Critical Dictionary of Jungian Analysis*
Authenticity	Being honest and open with children and other members of the staff team.
	Being honest about one's own feelings and vulnerabilities.
	Children need to be offered honesty and truthfulness in the responses from the adults around them if they are to best make sense of their world.
Being and becoming	Playing is of the moment, it is *Now* – it has no concern for the past or future, it is fundamentally ontological, concerned with the nature of being.
	In that each individual 'knows' what it is to be themselves, they are experts in their own being and therefore their own playing – any results emerging from that playing may never be predicted or controlled; the child's becoming is therefore also bound up with that 'beingness'. This is a position that is at odds with the dominant western paradigm of adult instruction, teaching, or the 'ages and stages' that pigeonhole children into categories of normality.

Child's evaluation of the return   The child's evaluation of the return may produce a response that extends the play, reduces or ends it, or is neutral. Again, the likely choice by the child and the intent of the play cannot be known by the adult. The child may choose to:

- respond to the play return – and so continue or broaden the theme of the play; play flow is established
- annihilate or end the play cycle – the process has produced what was necessary
- repeat the original play cue – to see what happens.

Containment   Holding the play for the child until they are able to return to the playing form.

The support that adults/workers can give to children in play should include the ability to hold, or 'contain', the play. It is about supporting a child through their initial tentative play cues, giving back a return to help the play on its way. It may also be about holding the frame while the child is away from the play (or when the play ends for the day).

Our professional containment is a crucial element of our working practice, knowing where boundaries are between play and non-play.

Contamination   Contamination in play occurs when the children's freely chosen play is affected adversely by the actions or comments of others (usually adults). Contamination may occur through concerns about safety, expected compliance with cultural norms, or through an attempt to guide or teach the child how to play or behave.

Daemon/demon   'Daemon'—the Greek word that in classical mythology refers to 'god within', one's inner deity or guiding spirit, also known as a genii or jinn, the tutelary deity or genius of a person; one's daemon or genii is also said to be synonymous with one's fate or fortune.

. . . But there is a strange and horrible thing about one's daemon: When honoured and acted upon, it is indeed one's guiding spirit; those who bear a god within bring genius to their work. When, however, one's daemon is heard but unheeded, it is said that the daemon becomes a demon, or evil spirit – divine energy and talent degenerates into self-destructive activity.

Ken Wilber (1991: 58) *Grace and Grit*

(Continued)

Term	Definition
Dysplay	Dysplay is apparent when play cues are laden with anxiety; the urgent, frantic play cues offered by children who are unable to complete the play cycle effectively.
	Children denied choice will be inhibited in their play, the cycle will be incomplete. The play drive will try to compensate with cues that are more urgent or aberrant, perhaps causing conflict with the environment around the child.
False self	There is a 'false self which develops on a compliance basis and is related in a passive way to the demands of external reality . . . the false self becomes organized to keep the world at bay, and there is another true self hidden away and therefore protected'.
	D.W. Winnicott (1988) *Human Nature*
Holistic play See also **Integral Play Framework**	Like all humans, the playing child has an experience of the world that is both emotional and physical at the same time; we live at the boundary of the personal and shared worlds. And, as has been commented by many writers, the integrated model recognizes that humans create their own world in relation to that of other people; humans are social animals who see their identity and status in relation to others.
	It should be noted that these are mutual worlds, different sides of a similar coin – humans shape and are shaped by their lived experience of mind, body and environment, as they integrate their different experiences of the world, which has an effect on who they are and become.
Integral Play Framework	The Integral Play Framework balances the experiences of the child in the tangible world of structures with the insubstantial world of feelings and beliefs. As children are playing they are using their bodies to move through and experience the world, either solitarily or with others. Those sensations are processed internally and inform the child's self-awareness, feelings and beliefs, which may be shared with others.
	For example; a group of children are playing chase, a physical game involving running around on the ground and over obstacles to evade capture. Ethan is 'it'; he is trying hard to pass the role to another and races round energetically. Initially frustrated that he cannot catch the others, he becomes elated when he tags his friend Sohail and manages to escape on to a high platform. Later he and Sohail talk about the game and what it felt like to be 'on' and what it was like when they were running away.

Integrity of intervention

Integrity of intervention is where the adult/worker is aware of the interventions they may need to make in a play session in order to make it as playful as possible.

The adult may be involved in disputed or conflicting frames – and may be called on to make judgements affecting the play frames of several children, or may need to remind a child of the risks taken when crossing boundaries. Where possible, the adult/worker should aim to offer a response that is playful rather than controlling or prescriptive.

Intervention – ludocentric

The four levels of intervention are *ludocentric* (play-centred) in their intent.

(1) Play maintenance:

The play is self-contained – no intervention is necessary, the adult/worker observes the activity.

(2) Simple involvement:

The adult acts as a resource for the play – this may be subtle, as in making a tool available for use, or more overt when responding to a request from children.

(3) Medial intervention:

At the request of the child, the adult becomes involved in the play – such as by offering alternatives from which the child chooses, or by initiating a game then withdrawing.

(4) Complex intervention:

There is a direct and extended overlap between playing children and the adult – the adult may need to take on a role in the play, or act as a partner to the playing child.

Intervention – safety

There will, of course, be times when the duty of care requires adults/workers to behave in a non-ludocentric manner – for example, when a child is in imminent danger of seriously harming themselves or others. Professional judgements on when to make such a non-ludocentric intervention will be informed by the adult/worker's level of understanding of how their play plays through them as adults and on their knowledge of the child/ren and the contexts and their instant risk assessment.

Life-world

The life-world is the psychic script by which people describe their own life and experience, the stories they tell themselves and others about their 'selfs' (as known).

(Continued)

Term	Definition
'Lila'	Lila is the spirit of divine play, seen in the urge to invent, to create. In Hinduism, all reality is seen as the outcome of creative play by the divine spirit.
Ludic	Playful.
Ludic consciousness	With a ludic consciousness might be perceived the child's play universe and the meeting with the external world as a flexible, holistic and ludic process.
	This totality is seen as being a psychic, non-physical, ludic ecology. By 'reading' the inherent encounter and the subsequent balancing, the resulting adaption and adjustment processes, practitioners can contribute to the child's development in a way that is child-centred, and encourage the self-healing potentials of play to take effect.
Ludic ecology	The ludic ecology is the space for play (both physical and psychic); not a solid formation, it is rather a fluid and supple projection; it is a mobile, flexible extension, where options, ideas and themes change and adapt in contact with the surrounding, and containing, environment.
Ludic third	The ludic process reflects the interplay of three subjectivities: the subjectivity of the child, of the adult and of the ludic third. The ludic third is a creation of the first player and the second player and, at the same time, the players are created by the ludic third (after Ogden 1994: 93). The adult/worker is aware of the ludic third when they are *self-witnessing*.
Ludido See also **Play drive**	The ludido, the play drive, could be precisely seen as the active agency of an evolving consciousness – such a description is closer to the definitions out of eastern psychologies and traditions, the *lila* principle – in what is called a 'field' or psychic, ludic ecology.
	The ludido functions through an interplay with surrounding 'fields' to circulate through the metalude, contained reality, and constructed reality, seeking, desiring animation, authority and law, text and context, æffective outlet, expression as a means of homeostasis. Sturrock (1996)
Ludocentric	The ludocentric (play-centred) model represents a process-based approach, and rests on the premise that potential benefit, both immediate and long term, derives from the ludic process itself. From this premise, therefore, the professional task of the adult is to support that play process. Any attempt to direct or control the play process has the potential to adulterate it and in so doing invalidate any benefit that might accrue.

Ludogogic   Of, pertaining to, or characteristic of a *ludogogue* or *ludogogy*.

Having the office or character of a ludogogue – that is, a person who arrives at insight in play and playing by virtue of self-witnessing and reflection.

Ludogogue   A ludogogue is an adult attendant to the child at play; a person who arrives at insight in play and playing by virtue of self-witnessing and reflection. A playing participant. A *play leader*, usually adult – in the sense that the commencing interpretation or analysis of any play expressions from the child/children is played through the adults first. The 'leading' is not of the play of the child, except when invited to do so, or where a 'role' requires the adult to do so – for example, in the ludic third . . . The leading is of the adult's own material as the basis for analysis. The 'This-is-how-it-plays-through-me' self-witnessing paradigm.

(Sturrock (2003), from Latin, *ludo* ('I play') + Greek, *ag gos* ('leader', from *agein*, 'to lead'))

Ludogogy   The function, profession or practice of a *ludogogue*.

The study of the science and art of the *ludogogue* through *self-witnessing* and *reflection*; education and training in the practice of a ludogogue.

Metalude   The metalude is the source point and beginning of the function of internalized gestalt formation within the play process. It describes the moment of daydreaming or reverie that sets out the intent of the play. The metalude is the 'unconsciously conscious' thought that precedes any playful act. It is formed in the internal world of the child from which *play cues* go into the external, physical world.

The term metalude also suggests the 'playfulness of play' in that it crosses boundaries and motifs in microseconds.

Mindfulness   'Moment-to-moment awareness' – being present in the moment, aware of what is happening Now, both within and outside of the self.

After Kabat-Zinn (1991)

(*Continued*)

Term	Definition
Modes of expression	The four major modes of expression, which children explore through their play that are developmental, inclusive and overlapping, are: the psychological (cognitive), the cultural (culture), the physical (science), the social (politics).

Primary mode	Major modes	Modes of expression
Subjective/ felt	Psychological	Instinctual, impulsive, emotional, symbolic, problem solving
	Cultural	Creativity, art, drama, music, belief, cultural understanding
Objective/ fact	Physical	Exploration, working with materials and the natural elements, movement skills, tactile skills, mastery
	Social	Exerting personal choice, cooperative play, social, legal and political skills

Term	Definition
Paraludic	Paraludic is playing alongside the child/ren and also playing alongside the internal ludic response to the children; an objective awareness of subjective playing.

In this mode, the adult is fully conscious of how the children's play expressions are 'playing through' them; they acknowledge this but do not privilege their needs over the child's. They engage *paraludically* in the play frame, for example, playing the great monster that the children want to chase them, but not using this role for their own ends, e.g. to dominate the child or to help them learn a lesson about strangers. |
| **Peak experiences**
See also **Translation** and **Transformation** | Peak experiences are especially joyous and exciting moments in life, involving sudden feelings of intense happiness and well-being, wonder and awe, and possibly also involving an awareness of transcendental unity or knowledge of higher truth (as though perceiving the world from an altered, and often vastly profound and awe-inspiring, perspective).

In play children may often have experiences that offer such feelings, however it may be many years before they are able to integrate the skills and knowledge necessary to replicate those moments at will.

After Abram Maslow (1964) *Religions, Values, and Peak Experiences* |

PISCES	PISCES was intended to be a rich acronym to help with thinking about play and the adult's role:

P – Play; Personal; Participation; Process; Physical; Psychic; Perspective

I – Identity; Intelligence; the workers, the child, site

S – Symbolic; Spiritual; Self; *Socius*, 'The community that holds our identity'

C – Creativity; Considerative Craft; Culture; Child, the workers and the site; wider Culture; Contemplation; Celebration

E – Ecology; Environment; Events; Experiences

S – Security; Safety of the site and the people who work there; of the workers' practice and their operative concerns

Gordon Sturrock (1997) *SPICE – a Redundant Metaphor: Towards a More Extensive Definition*

Play cues — The play cue is the signal the child gives that they want to play. This cue may be spoken, eye contact, a body signal or by the use of materials. The play cue comes from the thoughts of the child, their internal world, into the physical world, in the expectation of getting a response. A child kicking a ball towards another is a play cue; they are expected to kick it back. Picking up a paintbrush, singing a song and starting a conversation could all be play cues. Children invite participation by other children or adults in their play by communicating feelings, thoughts and intentions. And of course these cues may not always be seen as positive in effect.

Play cycle
Or play process — The play cycle consists of the full exchange of play from the child's first play cue, the establishment of the play frame, the perceived return from the outside world, the child's response to the return, and the further development of play to the point where the play is complete and so ended or annihilated.

Play drive or impulse
See also **Ludido** — The child's play drive or instinct, which functions through an interplay with surrounding 'fields' to circulate through the metalude, the impulse to play will be affected by the child's sense of identity and power (or lack of power), values, beliefs, level of thought and understanding, physical skill and ability. This drive to play is internal to the child and is manifested in the *play cue*.

(Continued)

Term	Definition
Play flow	Play flow occurs when the frame has been established and the child becomes 'lost' in their play. Children at play are 'alive in the moment', with no concern for the past or future. The play may cover a number of topics in a few moments, with roles changing, ideas developing and concepts shifting, or it could be the single focus on a particular aspect. The play becomes self-regulated and the adult/worker if not actually playing with the child is largely outside of the *play frame*. Once entered into, this play flow can absorb the child or children for minutes, or perhaps days, at a time.
Play frames	The play frame is a boundary, material or non-material, that keeps the play intact. The child may then change the frame by including others, moving objects or adapting it in some other way to create a varied response that maintains the play flow. The play frame is chosen and initiated by the child and is the enclosure for their imaginal expression. It will be supported or contained by the physical boundaries of the available play space, but the frame is not dependent upon and may or may not synchronize with those boundaries.
Play return **(play response)**	The play return is the response the child experiences as a result of the *play cue*. The play return will be found by the playing child from the environment or as initiated by another child or adult. It is what goes back to the child after they issue the play cue. The child will choose what to 'play' with. The return will usually come back from another child or adult; they will be playing together, though the child can also find a return from the environment around them. They may be digging for treasure in the sandpit; they may be hunting for insects in the bushes. If the child gets a positive response they may choose to extend and enhance that experience by issuing another cue; they will be playing and learning. If the child gets a negative response they may stop playing or try another play cue. Understanding this process helps the adult/worker offer choices to the child to help them play. When the return is initiated by an adult, it should be made with an awareness of the child's emotional state, cultural understanding, physical abilities and sense of power (as far as they can be known) and primarily the adult's own cultural understanding and sense of power.

Playing through us

Playing through us is the recognition that, when in the child play space, the adult is also engaging with the ludic material that emerges; it will trigger responses that the adult may be aware – or unconscious – of.

It is in the overlap of the two ludic fields that the locus of well-being is situated, for both child and adult.

In the first instance, the children's play is not adulterated by an immediate rush to judgement. The deliberations arrived at have a prophylactic distance applied that protects the child's rights to forms of playing, which are, for them, personally significant. The privileging of the child's being and becoming is maintained. Second, the interpretations derived from internalized processing of the attendant adult's own ludic material can, over time, be exercised into permitting personal self-understandings and awarenesses to be explored, creating not inconsiderable well-being.

Psycholudics

Psycholudics is the study of the mind and psyche at play, and describes the process of play as it happens. It proposes that play is essentially spiritually, ecologically and ontologically developmental.

Reflection – before and after play

Reflection – before and after play – includes a regular review of the work practice, both before and after the session.

This reflection should also include the practitioner's own behaviours and attitudes. It examines the themes and material that could not be predicted. Workers will form quick judgements about what to do in the play space. After the session, reflection will help with understanding the worker's judgement at that time.

Reflective continuum

See also
Association and amplification

The reflective continuum involves an awareness of both self and self-reflection that goes beyond the merely mechanistic recording of data. It is reflection in the moment, 'reflection in action' and reflection after the event, 'reflection on action' in order to become a better practitioner and a better person (after Schön 1983).

Self-witnessing

Self-witnessing is where the worker reflects on their practice from the *witness position*; the analysis of the self in relation to a relationship with a playing child.

This witnessing issues from a position where the reactions of the worker are the object of scrutiny.

(Continued)

Term	Definition
Transformation *Transcendence*	Generally read as 'change or alteration', transformation is to go beyond a prior form or state of oneself (Wilber 1980). In play children may go beyond previous levels of experience, in each of the four realms of self, physical body, cultural and social relationships. In transformation, new skill/knowledge is acquired that could not have occurred beforehand, yet with the retention of the previous knowledge or state of experience. For example, when children learn to walk they are still able to crawl, when they learn to relate to strangers, they can still relate to family members and friends.
Translation	Translation is a term defined by Wilber (1980) to indicate those states of experience where the self is simply given a new way to think or feel about reality, but that ultimately does not lead to transformation or change. For example, no matter how much individuals play with 'world making' games such as *Sim City*™, they cannot be fully equipped for life in the real world, relating to real people; the more successful an individual becomes at a given sport, it does not indicate that they will become more tolerant of others or self-reflective.
Unplayed-out material	Unplayed-out material is the dormant yet laden play impulses of adults that may manifest in play interchanges with children; if not recognized and dealt with, this may result in adulteration of the children's play, as it takes on greater meaning for the adult than the child. 'Being aware of our own unplayed-out material, recognizing it and acknowledging it, but not privileging it over the children's material, is what we mean by the intrasubjective application, it is to operate in the *witness position*. It is both ludocentric and paraludic and it has the potential to benefit both the children and ourselves.'
Witness position	Witness position is where the adult/worker is objectively (impartially) aware of their subjective relationship with another, in this case the playing child. Subjectivity often relies on thoughts and feelings of a personal nature; children will naturally act subjectively in their play. Practitioners need to act objectively (but not authoritatively) in relation to this emotional content; workers therefore need to be aware of their own affect and the impact of this material on their interactions and relationships. Therefore they need to 'witness' their own behaviour in the play space.

References

Argyris, C. and Schön, D. (1978) *Organization Learning: A Theory of Action Perspective*. Reading, MA: Addison Wesley.

Armitage, M. (2001) The ins and outs of school playground play: children's use of 'play places', in J. Bishop and M. Curtis (eds) *Play Today in the Primary School Playground*. Buckingham: Open University Press: 37–57.

Athey, C. (1990) *Extending Thought in Young Children: A Parent Teacher Partnership*. London: Paul Chapman.

Bassford Baker, K. (2012) Please don't help my kids, available at http://tiny.cc/lwzw1w.

Bates, C. (1999) *Play in a Godless World*. London: Open Gate Press.

Bateson, G. (1991) *A Sacred Unity: Further Steps to an Ecology of Mind*. New York: HarperCollins.

Bateson, P. and Martin, P. (2013) *Play, Playfulness, Creativity and Innovation*. Cambridge: Cambridge University Press.

BBC (2013) Cyber-blackmailers 'abusing hundreds of UK children', available at http://www.bbc.co.uk/news/uk-24163284.

Beckett, C., Maughan, B., Rutter, M., *et al.* (2006) Do the effects of early severe deprivation on cognition persist into early adolescence? Findings from the English and Romanian Adoptees Study, *Child Development*, 77(3): 696–711.

Bekoff, M. and Pierce, J. (2009) *Wild Justice: The Moral Lives of Animals*. Chicago: University of Chicago Press.

Bird, W. (2007) *Natural Thinking: Investigating the Links between the Natural Environment, Biodiversity and Mental Health*. Sandy: RSPB, available at www.rspb.org.uk/policy/health.

Bjorkqvist, K., Lagerspetz, K.M.J. and Kaukiainen, A. (1991) Do girls manipulate and boys fight? Developmental trends in regard to direct and indirect aggression, *Aggressive Behaviour*, 18: 117–127.

Bolton, G. (2010) *Reflective Practice: Writing and Professional Development*. London: Sage Publications.

Bronfenbrenner, U. (1979) *The Ecology of Human Development*. Cambridge, MA: Harvard University Press.

Brown, S. (2009) *Play: How it Shapes the Brain, Opens the Imagination and Invigorates the Soul*. London: Penguin Avery.

Bruce, T. (2001) *Learning through Play, Babies, Toddlers and the Foundation Years*. London: Hodder Education.

Bruce, T. (ed.) (2006) *Early Childhood – A Guide for Students*. London: Sage Publications.

Burghardt, G. (2005) *The Genesis of Animal Play: Testing the Limits*. Boston, MA: MIT Press.

Byron, T. (2008) *Safer Children in a Digital World: The Report of the Byron Review*. Nottingham: DCSF Publications.

CABE (2004) *Involving Young People in the Design and Care of Urban Spaces*. CABE Space and CABE Education.

Caillois, R. (1961) *Man, Play and Games*. New York: Simon & Schuster.

Campbell, D. (2013) Doctors sound alarm on child fitness and health, *Guardian*, 21 August.

Campbell, M.A. (2007) Cyber bullying and young people: treatment principles not simplistic advice, available at www.scientist-practitioner.com, paper of the week, 23 February.

Carlile, O. and Jordan, A. (2012) *Approaches to Creativity: A Guide to Teachers*. Buckingham: Open University Press.

Carr, M. (2001) *Assessment in Early Childhood Settings: Learning Stories*. London: Sage Publications.

Casey, T. (2007) *Environments for Outdoor Play*. London: Paul Chapman.

Cassidy, T., Rushe, J. and Giles, M. (2010) *Patterns of Play as a Child and Long Term Health*. British Psychological Society/University of Ulster.

Chomsky, N. (1965) *Aspects of the Theory of Syntax*. Cambridge, MA: MIT Press.

Child in the City (2012) Available at http://tiny.cc/gp0d2w.

Child Poverty Action Group (2009) Available at http://tiny.cc/bovq4w.

Clark, A. and Moss, P. (2001) *Listening to Young Children: The Mosaic Approach*. London: National Children's Bureau for the Joseph Rowntree Foundation.

Csikszentmihalyi, M. (1990) *Flow – The Psychology of Optimal Experience*. New York: Harper & Row.

Cui, M., Yang, Y., Yang, J., *et al.* (2006) Enriched environment experience overcomes the memory deficits and depressive-like behavior induced by early life stress, *Neuroscience Letters*, 404: 208–212.

Darwin, J. (2010) *Mindfulness and Situation Awareness*. Sheffield: Centre for Individual and Organisational Development.

de Bono, E. (1991) *Handbook for the Positive Revolution*. London: Penguin Books.

de Bono, E. (1992) *Serious Creativity: Using the Power of Lateral Thinking to Create New Ideas*. London: HarperCollins.

Denscombe, M. (2003) *The Good Research Guide* (2nd edn). Buckingham: Open University Press.

Diamond, A. (2007) Interrelated and interdependent, *Developmental Science*, 10(1): 152–158.

Edelman, G. (2006) *Second Nature: Brain Science and Human Knowledge*. Boston, MA: Yale University Press.

Else, P. (1999) Practical applications of the pscholudic model for play work, in *Therapeutic Playwork Reader 1: 1995–2000*. Eastleigh: Common Threads.

Else, P. (2008) *Maximising Play Value*, unpublished.

Else, P. (2009) *The Value of Play*. London: Continuum.

Else, P. (2013) Beauty of play, *Ludemos* website, available at http://tiny.cc/aiy65w.

Else, P., Le Fevre, D. and Wolstenholme, C. (2010) *Everybody In: A Report on the Application of New Games in a School Setting*. Sheffield: Sheffield Hallam University.

Eno, B. (1996) *A Year with Swollen Appendices*. London: Faber & Faber.

Fields in Trust (2008) *Planning and Design for Outdoor Sport and Play*. London: Fields in Trust/National Playing Fields Association.

Fjortoft, I. (2004) Landscape and play: the effects of natural environments on children's play and motor development, *Children, Youth and Environments*, 14(2): 21–44.

Flemmen, A. (2005) *Real Play – A Socio-Motor Behaviour*. Volda: Volda University College.

Flick, U. (2006) *An Introduction to Qualitative Research*. London: Sage.

Fox, M.J. (2002) *Lucky Man*. London: Ebury Press.

Gardner, D. (2008) *Risk: The Science and Politics of Fear*. London: Virgin Books.

Gardner, H. (1999) *Intelligence Reframed: Multiple Intelligences for the 21st Century*. New York: Basic Books.

Garvey, C. (1977) *Play*. Cambridge, MA: Harvard University Press.

Gibbs, G. (1988) *Learning by Doing: A Guide to Teaching and Learning Methods*. Oxford: Further Education Unit.

Gibson, J.J. (1977) The theory of affordances, in R. Shaw and J. Bransford (eds) *Perceiving, Acting, and Knowing*. New York: Basic Books.

Gordon, G. and Esbjorn-Hargens, S. (2007) Integral play: an exploration of the playground and the evolution of the player, *AQAL: Journal of Integral Theory and Practice*, 2(3): 62–104.

Gray, P. (2013) Play as preparation for learning and life, *American Journal of Play*, 5(3): 271–292.

Grieshaber, S. and McArdle, F. (2010) *The Trouble with Play*. Maidenhead: Open University Press: 60.

Griffiths, J. (2013) *Kith*. London: Hamish Hamilton.

Hall, G. (2007) Inside the theory of the U: interview with Peter Senge and Otto Scharmer, *Reflections*, 8(4), 6–11.

Holland, P. (2003) *We Don't Play with Guns Here: War, Weapon and Superhero Play in the Early Years*. Maidenhead: Open University Press.

Huffington Post (2013) Anne Frank's diary too 'pornographic', available at http://tiny.cc/a2xb2w.

Hughes, B. (1996a) *A Playworker's Taxonomy of Play Types*. Ely: Play Education.

Hughes, B. (1996b) *Play Environments: A Question of Quality*. London: Playlink.

Hughes, B. (2002) *A Playworker's Taxonomy of Play Types* (2nd edn). Ely: Play Education.

Hughes, B. (2006) *Play Types – Speculations and Possibilities*. London: London Centre for Playwork Education and Training.

Hughes, B. (2012) *Evolutionary Playwork; Reflective Analytic Practice* (2nd edn). London: Routledge.

Hughes, B. and King, F. (1984) *The Salmon Book*. JNCTP.

Huizinga, J. (1950) *Homo Ludens*. London: Routledge & Kegan Paul.

Ip-Dip 74 (2011) *Ip-Dip 74. Ip-Dip for Professionals in Play*. Eastbourne: Playwork Development and Training CIC Company No: 6765978.

Ip-Dip 75 (2011) *Ip-Dip 75. Ip-Dip for Professionals in Play*. Eastbourne: Playwork Development and Training CIC Company No: 6765978.

Jennings, S. (1995) Playing for real, *International Play Journal*, 3: 132–141.

Jesson, J. (2012) *Developing Creativity in the Primary School*. Maidenhead: Open University.

Johns, C. (2000) *Becoming a Reflective Practitioner*. Oxford: Blackwell Science.

Johnson, M.H. (2008) Brain development in childhood: a literature review and synthesis for the Byron Review on the impact of new technologies on children, available at http://www.eye-pat.org/login/uploaded/JohnsonBrainDevelopmentLiterature ReviewfortheByronReview.pdf.

Jung, C.G. (1938) Psychology and religion, *Collected Works 11: Psychology and Religion: West and East*. New York: Pantheon.

Kabat-Zinn, J. (1991) *Full Catastrophe Living: Using the Wisdom of Your Body and Mind to Face Stress, Pain, and Illness*. New York: Delta Trade.

Kagen, R. (1982) *The Evolving Self: Problem and Process in Human Development*. London: Harvard University Press.

Kolb, D.A. (1984) *Experiential Learning*. New York: Prentice Hall.

Kolb, D.A. and Fry, R. (1975) Toward an applied theory of experiential learning, in C. Cooper (ed.) *Theories of Group Process*. London: John Wiley.

Konner, M. (2010) *The Evolution of Childhood*. Cambridge, MA: Belknap Press.

Koestler, A. (1967) *The Ghost in the Machine*. London: Penguin.

Ladoon, B. (n.d.) Available at http://tiny.cc/11zw1w.

Lansdown, G. (2013) *United Nations Convention on the Rights of the Child – General Comment No. 17 (2013) on Article 31*, available at http://www2.ohchr.org/english/bodies/crc/comments.htm.

Lee, L. (1959) *Cider with Rosie*. London: Hogarth Press.

Lester, S. (2010) Play and ordinary magic: the everydayness of play, *Playwork London Conference*, available at http://tiny.cc/iasd2w.

Lester, S. and Russell, W. (2008) *Play for a Change*. London: NCB.

Lester, S. and Russell, W. (2010) *Children's Right to Play: An Examination of the Importance of Play in the Lives of Children Worldwide, Working Paper no. 57*. The Hague, NL: Bernard van Leer Foundation.

Maine Melis, C. and Ronson, S. (2006) Ideas are born in fields of play: towards a theory of play and creativity in organizational settings, in *Research in Organizational Behavior: An Annual Series of Analytical Essays and Critical Reviews Research in Organizational Behavior*, volume 27: 81–131.

Maslow, A. (1964) *Religions, Values and Peak Experiences*. New York: Penguin.

McGonigal, J. (2011) *Reality is Broken*. London: Jonathan Cape.

McLellan, V. (1998) *Wise Words and Quotes*. Colorado Springs, CO: Tyndale.

Meares, R. (1992) *The Metaphor of Play*. Melbourne: Hill of Content.

Merleau-Ponty, M. (1948) *The World of Perception*. Abingdon: Routledge.

Metro (2013) Children get police warning letters for 'intimidating' and 'antisocial' behaviour because they played outside, available at http://tiny.cc/skx21w.

Millar, S. (1968) *The Psychology of Play*. London: Penguin Books.

Momlogic (2009) Available at http://tiny.cc/orb65w.

Moon, J.A. (2006) *Learning Journals: A Handbook for Academics, Students and Professional Development*. London: Kogan Page.

Moore, R. (1986) *Childhood's Domain: Play and Place*. London: Croom Helm.

NASP (2006) Shoplifting statistics, National Association for Shoplifting Prevention, available at http://tiny.cc/6bnh2w.

National Obesity Observatory (2013) *National Child Measurement Programme: Changes in Children's Body Mass Index between 2006/07 and 2011/12*, available at http://tiny.cc/1clw2w.

NCB (2008) *Quality in Play*. London: National Children's Bureau/Play England.

NCB (2010) *A Journey NOT a Destination*. London: NCB/Play England.

Neil, S. (2013) Personal communication.

Nicholson, S. (1971) How not to cheat children: the theory of loose parts, *Landscape Architecture Quarterly*, 62(1): 30–34.

NPFA/CPC/Playlink (2000) *Best Play*. London: National Playing Fields Association, Children's Play Council, Playlink.

Ofcom (2011) *Children and Parents: Media Use and Attitudes Report*, available at http://stakeholders.ofcom.org.uk/binaries/research/media-literacy/oct2011/Children_and_parents.pdf.

Ofcom (2012) *Children and Parents: Media Use and Attitudes Report*, available at http://tiny.cc/xe51cx.

Ogden, T.H. (1994) *Subject of Analysis*. London: Karnac Books.

Opie, I. and Opie, P. (1959) The Lore and Language of Schoolchildren. Oxford: Oxford University Press.

Panksepp, J. (2001) The long-term psychobiological consequences of infant emotions: prescriptions for the twenty-first century, *Infant Mental Health Journal*, 22(1–2): 132–173.

Parenting by the Minute (2010) Disney taught my kids bad words, available at http://tiny.cc/6enh2w.

Parten, M. (1932) Social participation among preschool children, in *Journal of Abnormal and Social Psychology*, 28(3): 136–147.

Parkes, A., Sweeting, H., Wight, D. and Henderson, M. (2013) Do television and electronic games predict children's psychosocial adjustment? Longitudinal research using the UK Millennium Cohort Study, *Archives of Disease in Childhood*, 98: 341–348.

Pellis, S. and Pellis, V. (2009) *The Playful Brain: Venturing to the Limits of Neuroscience*. Oxford: OneWorld.

Phillips, A. (1998) *The Beast in the Nursery*. London: Faber & Faber.

Phillips, A. (2005) *Going Sane*. London: Penguin.

Philpot, J. (2013) Personal Communication.

Piaget, J. (1962) *Play, Dreams and Imitation in Childhood*. London: Routledge.

Pink, D. (2010) *Drive: The Surprising Truth About What Motivates Us*. London: Canongate Books.

Play Wales (2013) *The Role of Adults in Children's Play*. Cardiff: Play Wales.

PPSG – Playwork Principles Scrutiny Group (2005) *Playwork Principles*. Cardiff: Play Wales, available at http://www.playwales.org.uk/eng/playworkprinciples.

Ramsden, P. (1988) Studying learning: improving teaching, in P. Ramsden (ed.) *Improving Learning: New Perspectives*. London: Kogan Page.

Ransome, A. (1930) *Swallows and Amazons*. London: Jonathan Cape.

Robinson, K. (2009) *The Element: How Finding Your Passion Changes Everything*. London: Penguin.

Robinson, K. (2011) *Out of Our Minds: Learning to be Creative* (2nd edn). London: Capstone.

Rogers, C. (1961) *On Becoming a Person: A Therapist's View of Psychotherapy*. London: Constable.

Rolfe, G., Freshwater, D. and Jasper, M. (2001) *Critical Reflection in Nursing and the Helping Professions: A User's Guide*. Basingstoke: Palgrave Macmillan.

Roosevelt, T. (1907) Letter to Washington Playground Association, February 16, 1907, *Presidential Addresses and State Papers*: 1163.

Rowan, D. (2005) Have children really forgotten how to play?, *The Times Magazine*, 21 May.

Russell, W. (2005) The unnatural art of playwork: BRAWGS continuum, in G. Sturrock and P. Else (eds) *Therapeutic Playwork Reader 2*. Sheffield: Ludemos.

Rutter, M. (2006) Implications of resilience concepts for scientific understanding, *Annals of the New York Academy of Sciences*, 1094: 1–12.

Sahlberg, P. (2012) *Finnish Lessons: What Can the World Learn from Educational Change in Finland?* New York: Teachers College Press.

Samuels, A., Shorter, B. and Plant, F. (1986) *A Critical Dictionary of Jungian Analysis*. London: Routledge.

Schön, D. (1983) *The Reflective Practitioner, How Professionals Think in Action*. New York: Basic Books.

Seligman M.E.P. (2002) *Authentic Happiness*. London: Nicholas Brealey.

Senge, P., Scharmer, C.O., Jaworski, J. and Flowers, B.S. (2005) *Presence: Exploring Profound Change in People, Organizations and Society*. London: Nicholas Brealey Publishing Ltd.

Siviy, S. (1998) Neurobiological substrates of play behaviour: glimpses into the structure and function of mammalian playfulness, in M. Bekoff and J.A. Byers (eds) *Animal Play: Evolutionary, Comparative and Ecological Perspectives*. Cambridge: Cambridge University Press.

Siviy, S.M. and Atrens, D.M. (1992) The energetic costs of rough-and-tumble play in the juvenile rat, *Developmental Psychobiology*, 25(2): 137–148.

Smith, P.K. (2010) *Children and Play*. London: Wiley-Blackwell.

Spangler, D. (2008) A vision of holarchy, available at http://www.sevenpillarshouse. org/article/a_vision_of_holarchy1/.

Spencer, H. (1904) *An Autobiography*. London: Williams and Norgate.

Sturrock, G. (1996) A diet of worms, in *Therapeutic Playwork Reader 1* (2005). Southampton: Common Threads.

Sturrock, G. (1997) SPICE – A Redundant Metaphor: Towards a More Extensive Definition, in *Therapeutic Playwork Reader 1* (2005). Southampton: Common Threads.

Sturrock, G. (2003) The ludic third, in *Therapeutic Playwork Reader 2* (2005). Sheffield: Ludemos.

Sturrock, G. (2011) What play is, *Ip-Dip*, 74. Eastbourne: Meynell Games.

Sturrock, G. and Else, P. (1998) The playground as therapeutic space: playwork as healing, in *Therapeutic Playwork Reader 1* (2005). Southampton: Common Threads.

Sturrock, G. Russell, W. and Else, P. (2004) *Towards Ludogogy, Parts I, II and III. The Art of Being and Becoming through Play*. Sheffield: Ludemos.

Sutton-Smith, B. (1997) *The Ambiguity of Play*. London: Harvard University Press.

Swimme, B. (1984) *The Universe is a Green Dragon*. London: Arkana.

Sylva, K., Bruner, J.S. and Genova, P. (1976) The role of play in the problem-solving of children 3–5 years old, in J.S. Bruner, A. Jolly and K. Sylva (eds) *Play: Its Role in Development and Evolution*. New York: Basic Books: 244–257.

Tawil, B. (2012) Personal communication.

UNICEF (2007) *An Overview of Child Well-being in Rich Countries, Report Card 7*. Florence: Innocenti Research Centre.

UNICEF (2013) *Child Well-being in Rich Countries: A Comparative Overview, Report Card 11*. Florence: Innocenti Research Centre.

Vieira, M.L., Garcia, M.P., Rau, D.D. and Prado, A.B. (2005) Effects of different opportunities for social interaction on the play fighting behavior in male and female golden hamsters (*Mesocricetus auratus*), *Developmental Psychobiology*, 47(4): 345–353.

Vygotsky, L.S. (1976) Play and its role in the mental development of the child, in J.S. Bruner, A. Jolly and K. Sylva (eds) *Play – its Role in Development and Evolution*. New York: Basic Books.

Ward, C. (1978) *The Child in the City*. New York: Pantheon.

Webb, S. and Brown, F. (2003) Playwork in adversity: working with abandoned children in Romania, in F. Brown (ed.) *Playwork Theory and Practice*. Buckingham: Open University Press.

Weick, K.E. and Sutcliffe, K.M. (2007) *Managing the Unexpected*. London: John Wiley & Sons.

Welsh Assembly Government (2002) *Play Policy*. Cardiff: Welsh Assembly Government.

Welsh Government/Play Wales (2012) *Play Sufficiency Assessment Toolkit*. Cardiff: Welsh Government.

Wilber, K. (1980) *The Atman Project*. Wheaton, IL: Quest Books.

Wilber, K. (1991) *Grace and Grit*. Dublin: New Leaf.

Wilber, K. (1997) *The Eye of Spirit*. Boston, MA: Shambhala.

Wilber, K. (2000) Introduction, in *Collected Works of Ken Wilber, Volume 8*. Boston, MA: Shambhala.

Wild Network (2013) The Wild Network, available at 999http://projectwildthing.com/thewildnetwork.

Winnicott, D.W. (1990) *Human Nature*. London: Routledge.

Worthington, M. and Carruthers, E. (2006) Mathematical development, in T. Bruce (ed.) *Early Childhood – A Guide for Students*. London: Sage.

Yun, A., Bazar, K., Gerber, A., Lee, P. and Daniel, S. (2005) The dynamic range of biologic functions and variation of many environmental cues may be declining in the modern age: implications for diseases and therapeutics, *Medical Hypotheses*, 65(1): 173–178.

Index

A–Z OF PLAY IN EARLY CHILDHOOD

Janet Moyles

9780335246380 (Paperback)
2012

eBook also available

This indispensable guide uses a unique glossary format to explore some of the key themes in play in early childhood, many of which regularly arise for students, tutors, parents and practitioners. As well as covering key concepts, theories and influential figures in the field, the book considers important aspects of each construct and highlights the complexity of play in early childhood.

Key features:

- Split into a comprehensive glossary running through elements of play from A–Z, it is a useful, fun and unique companion to understanding children's play
- Original thoughts from well known early years people including Tricia David, Carol Aubrey, Angela Anning and Lilian Katz

www.openup.co.uk

RETHINKING SUPERHERO AND WEAPON PLAY
Superheroes and Children's Moral Development

Steven Popper

9780335247066 (Paperback)
April 2013

eBook also available

This book explores children's war, weapon and superhero play with a view to examining its potential (positive) impact on developing moral values and sensibilities, and to the many moral themes available for children's exploration during their engagement with such play, and the traditional and continuing need for children to receive a good moral education, with reference to many ideas from educational philosophy.

Key features:

- It links examples of children's real-life play and perspectives to theories about play, moral development and narrative psychology
- It explores the continuing attraction of classical dualism (i.e. good versus evil) for children and various educational perspectives about this
- Contains a wealth of learning opportunities and suggestions of ways to use superheroes to advance children's moral, philosophical and emotional thinking

www.openup.co.uk

 OPEN UNIVERSITY PRESS
McGraw - Hill Education

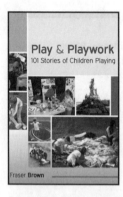

PLAY AND PLAYWORK
101 Stories of Children Playing

Fraser Brown

9780335244652 (Paperback)
September 2014

eBook also available

Children like to play. They get all sorts of benefits from playing.
They get the most benefit from play when they are in control of
what they are doing. Yet there are lots of circumstances today that
mean children are not able to control their own play and that's where
playwork comes in, where the role of the playworker is to create
environments that enable children to take control of their playing.

This book aims to explore the similarities, differences and
tensions that exist between play and playwork including appropriate
definitions and the conflict around the role of the adult. Fraser
Brown proposes a play to playwork continuum, where playing can be
considered a 'developmental and evolutionary' activity and playwork
a 'compensatory' activity.

Helpfully structured around the aspects considered by the author
as most important for playwork, this book uses 101 fascinating
stories of children playing to illuminate a range of play and
playwork theories. The rich array of powerful stories - drawn from
the casebooks of eminent and experienced playworkers - speak for
themselves whilst at the same time triggering theoretical explorations
that are interwoven with the stories in each chapter.

Mesmerizing, absorbing and original, this is essential reading
for playwork students and practitioners, as well as for students
and practitioners of early years, childhood, children's health and
wellbeing, and children's social care.

www.openup.co.uk

OPEN UNIVERSITY PRESS
McGraw - Hill Education